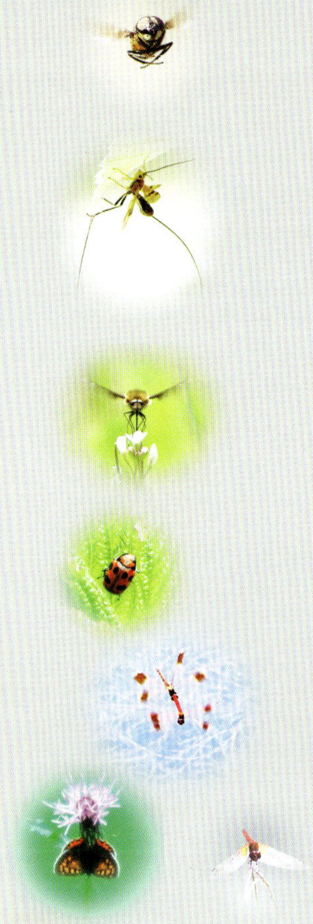

Japanese Insects and Haiku

虫の世界と五七五

A Photobook by

Seisui KIKUKAWA

菊川蜻水 写真集

Translation into English by

Tomoko YAMAMOTO

Yaeko Barre KOCHI

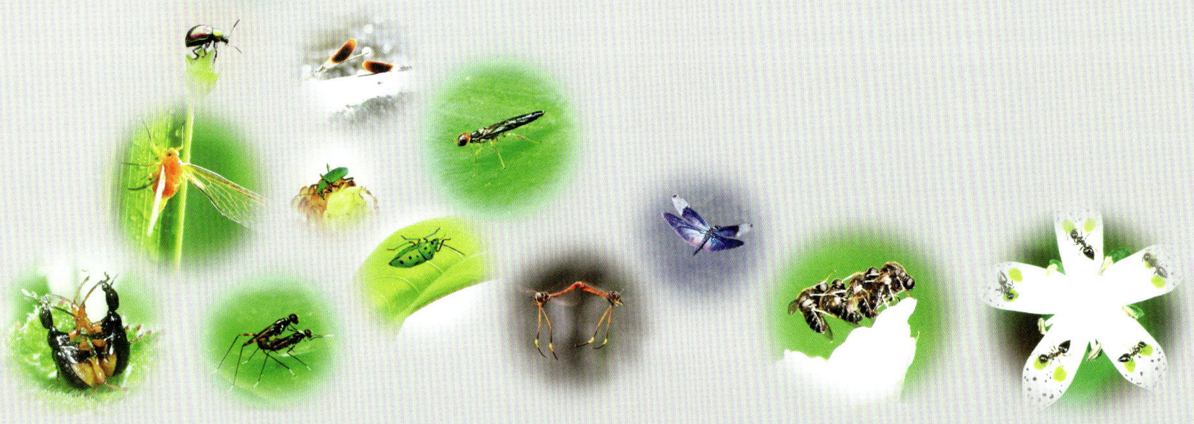

Index

インデックス

Cover: Larva of Holochlora japonica　表紙:クダマキモドキの一種の幼虫　Back Cover: Aciagrion migratum　裏表紙:ホソミイトトンボ

Shining Spring

春光る

A white-eye hops around twigs of cherry tree.

メジロは満開の花の中を
スキップします

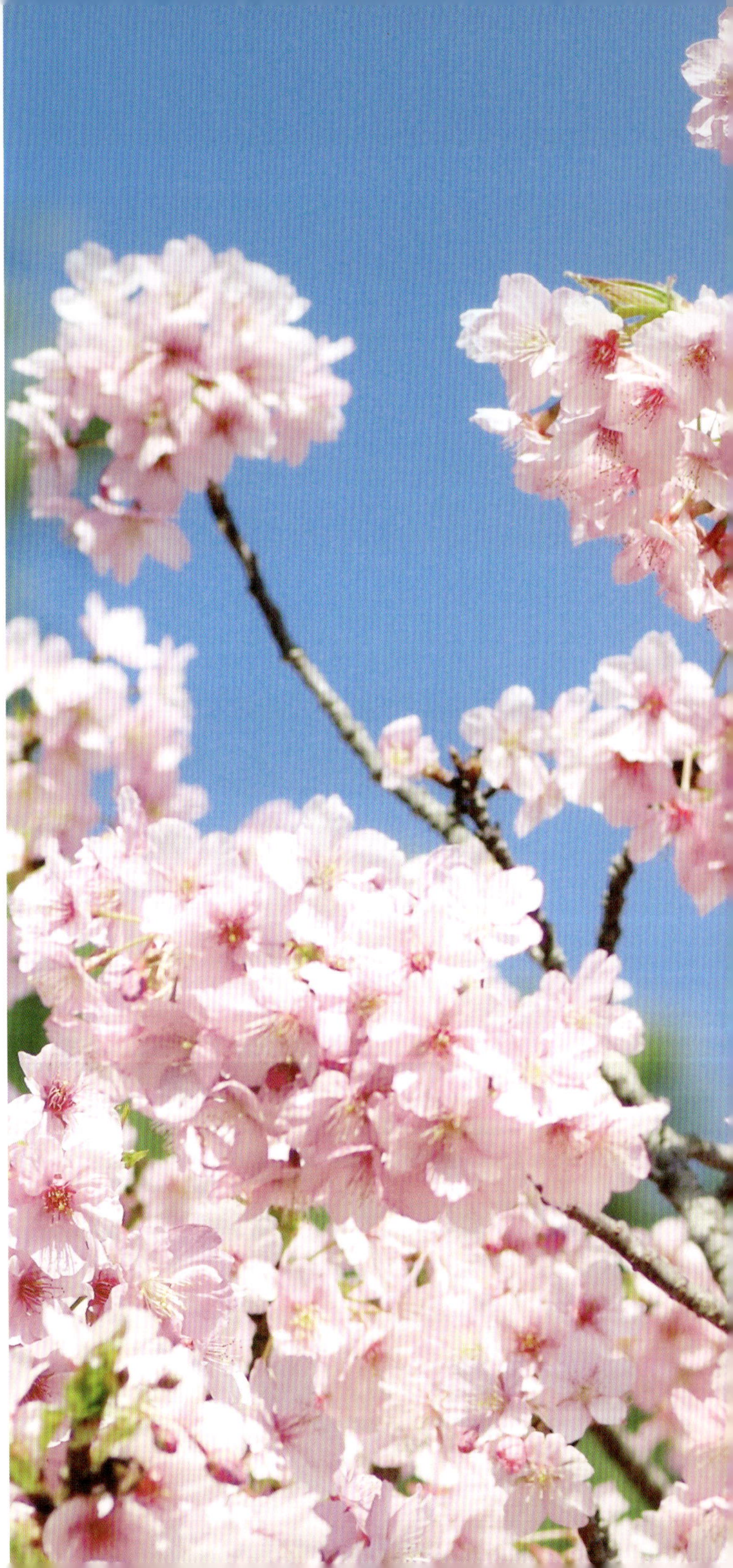

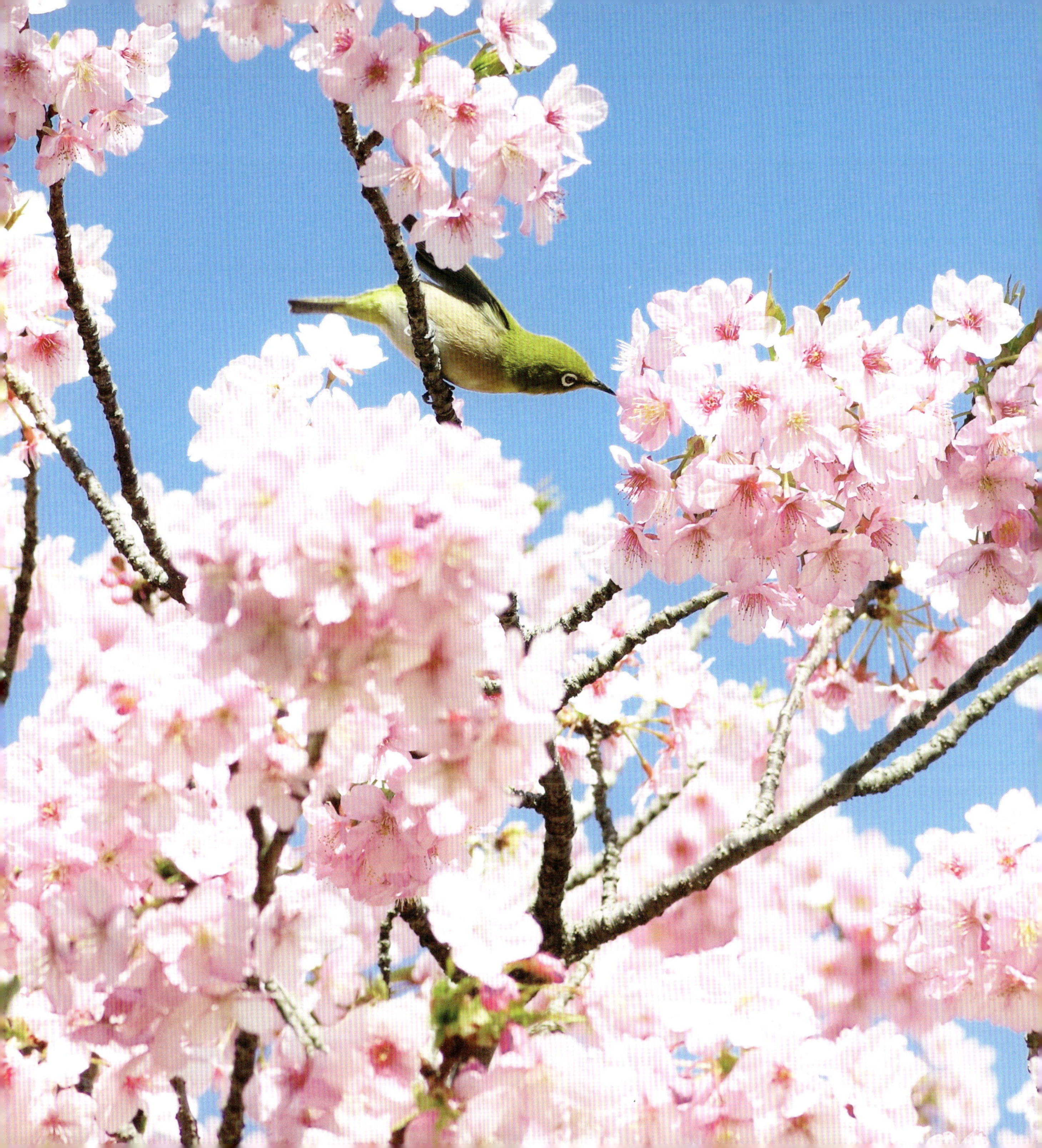

In the firmament
filled with plum's sweet fragrance
fluffy hoverflies enjoy the scent

空天に　梅の香みちて
ふわふわり

Walking in the spring afternoon sunlight,
I came across a plum tree already past bloom.
Gentle scents of plum blossoms filled the air with a lot of small fluffy insects in the sky.
When I magnified the picture, I found they were a kind of hoverflies.
They hardly changed their positions by moving skillfully their wings and bending their legs.
Their large stripe-patterned eyes are so fabulous.

昼下がりの野の小路を春の陽を楽しみながら歩いているとき、満開を過ぎた
梅の木の下を通りました。あたり一面にほんわかとしたやさしい香りがただよっていて、
空にはたくさんの小さな虫が浮かんでいます。写真を撮って拡大してみると、
ハナアブの一種のようです。脚を縮めて翅を上手に動かしてほとんど位置をかえません。
大きな縞模様の眼がすてきです。

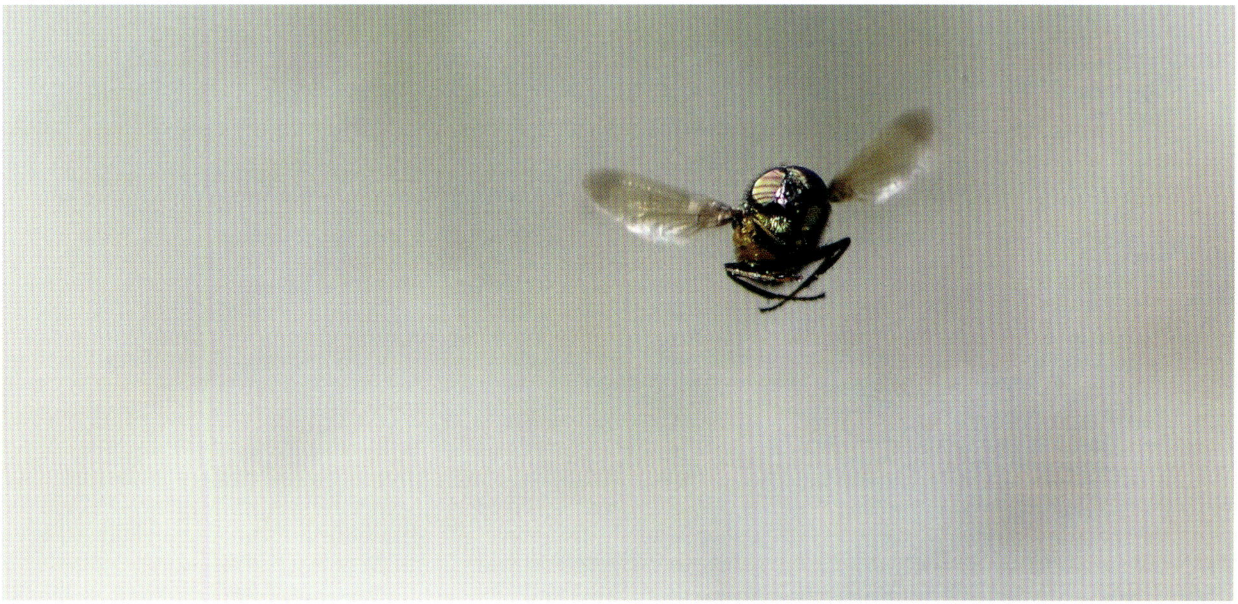

Syrphidae / Hoverfly (February, Kyushu)　ハナアブの一種（2月 鹿児島県）

In the verdant meadow
a crimson flower appears
as if twin-flowered

野はみどり　花はくれない
2輪咲き

There used to be a nationwide organization called *"Hana-no-kai"* (an association for flower photographers) led by photographer Shōtaro Akiyama. As a member of its Kagoshima branch, I was taking photos of flowers and insects with soft focus lens which was a fashion. Thistles were in full bloom after plum blossom season, with a number of butterflies flying around. I remember like yesterday the moment when I pressed the shutter button lying on the ground while minding bokeh. Small copper butterfly is a ubiquitous insect that helps me as a photo model anytime and anywhere.

秋山庄太郎先生の"花の会"という全国組織がありました。
私も鹿児島支部の一員で、はやりのソフトレンズ*[1]で花や虫を撮っていました。
花が終わったばかりの梅林にアザミが咲いていて、チョウたちもたくさんいます。
地面に腹ばいになって、ボケを気にしながらシャッターを押したのが昨日のことのようです。
ベニシジミはいつでもどこでもモデルになってくれる便利な被写体です。

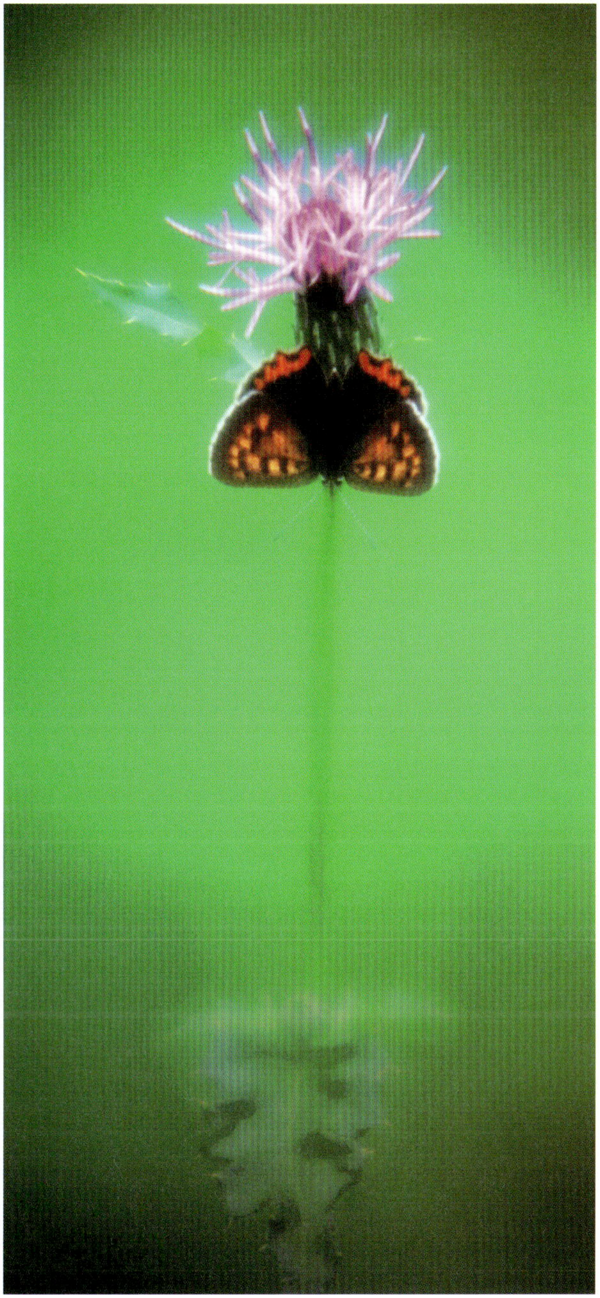

Lycaena phlaeas /
Small copper butterfly
(April, Kyushu)
ベニシジミ(4月 鹿児島県)

Soft and green palms
cradling so tenderly
tiny Hina doll

柔らかき　手にだかれおり
ひなだるま

A bright spring sun shines mountain path along the river.
Plants and trees are full of life with growing fresh green leaves.
I found something red and round on a strawberry leaf. It was so distinct even at a distance.
Leaf beetle. Its black-spotted red costume is often said to be a mimic of ladybird.
Living in the main island and Kyushu region, the species are often observed from spring to summer.
Their body length is about 5 mm and they eat leaves of fagaceae and rosaceous plants.

川沿いの山路は春の陽がいっぱい。草も木も新しい黄緑色の葉をのばして、
命の喜びであふれています。イチゴの葉の上に赤い丸いものを見つけました。
遠くからでもめだっています。赤い地に黒い点の衣裳は、テントウムシに擬態しているとも
言われます。本州から九州にすんでいて、春から夏に見かけることが多いようです。
体長５ミリほどで、ブナ科やバラ科の植物の葉を食べるそうです。

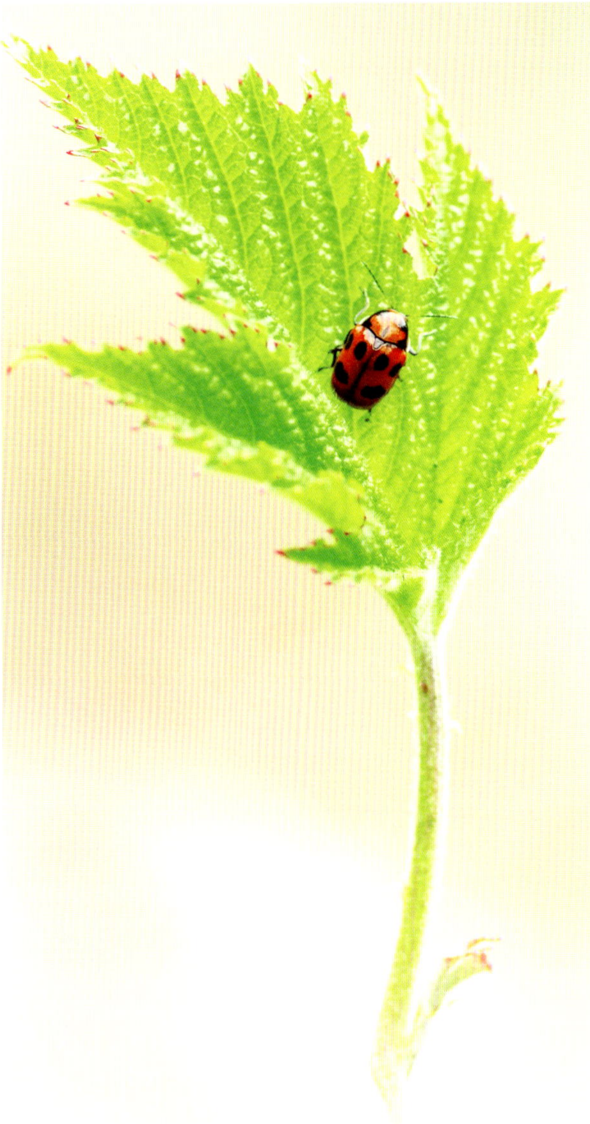

Cryptocephalus signaticeps /
Leaf beetle (April, Kyushu)
クロホシツツハムシ（4月 鹿児島県）

On wild strawberry
a little quartet
pushing back to back

草いちご　おしくらまんじゅう
4人組

White flowers of wild strawberry are blossoming in a dim forest.
A female hunchback fly comes to the flower, followed by males in a fuss trying to love her.
But they seem to have trouble distinguishing female from males. Because of their holoptic eyes,
they cannot see very well. In the photograph here, the one in front is female and others are males.
These quite stooped black flies are often likened to the Hunchback of Notre-Dame.
Their larvae grow inside spiders.

薄暗い林道に、草いちごの白い花が咲いています。そこにメスがやってくるとオスたちは大騒ぎ。
背中に乗ろうと懸命です。でもメスとオスの区別もつかないみたい。
左右の眼が合体していてよく見えないのかも。写真では、一番前がメスで後の3頭はオスです。
すごい猫背の黒っぽいアブで、ノートルダムのせむし男*2みたいだと形容されることも。
幼虫はクモの体内で成長するそうです。

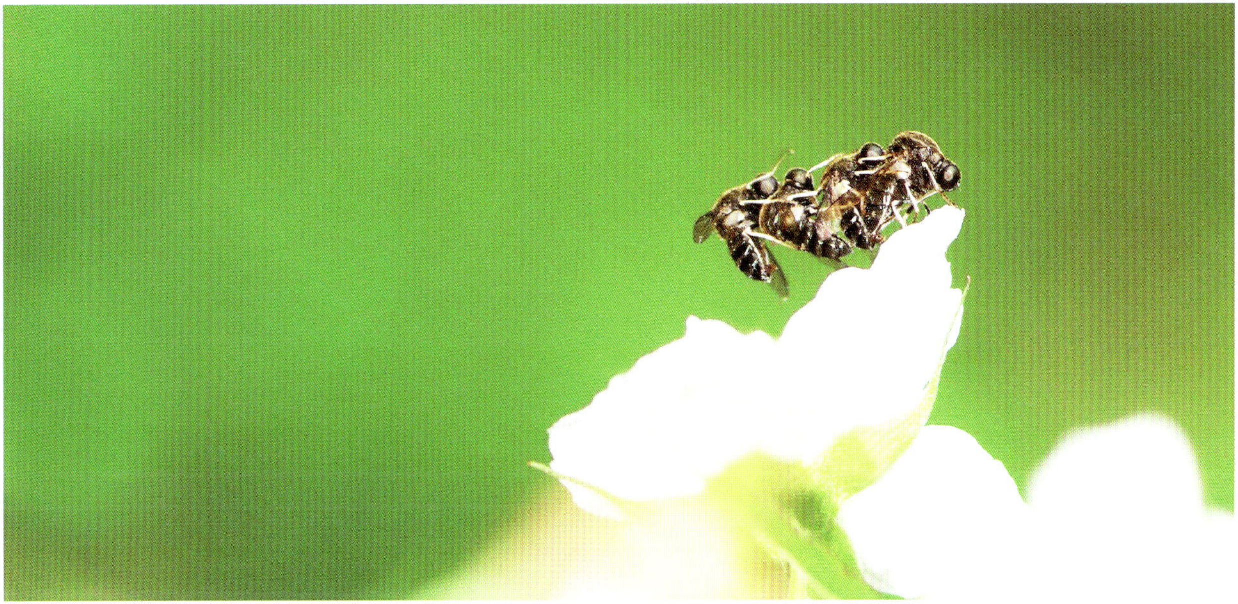

Oligoneura nigroaenea sp. / Hunchback fly (May, Kyushu)　セダカコガシラアブの一種（5月 鹿児島県）

Slowly and quietly awaiting under balmy breeze of May

そろそろと　五月の風を
さぐりおり

A friend of mine, also a big insect lover, told me his secret place where emergence of dragonfly can be seen.
The emergence is around holidays in May. Expecting of the big event, I went to the place and
found larva with its head out of hole. Dragonfly usually stays as larva for three to four years.
Their larval shells are often muddy because they live in holes they made in cliffs where water drips.
Males waylaying for females to come to lay eggs are placid and often rest on people's hats.
This Japanese endemic species live in the main island and Kyushu region.

虫友に教わった林道の崖では、連休のころに羽化が見られます。
もうそろそろかもと思って出かけたら、ヤゴが穴から顔を出していました。
幼虫の期間は3〜4年だそうです。水がしたたり落ちる崖に穴を掘って生活しているので、
羽化殻は泥だらけのことが多いです。産卵に来るメスを待ち伏せしているオスは、
おっとりしていて、帽子にとまったりします。日本特産種で本州と九州にすんでいます。

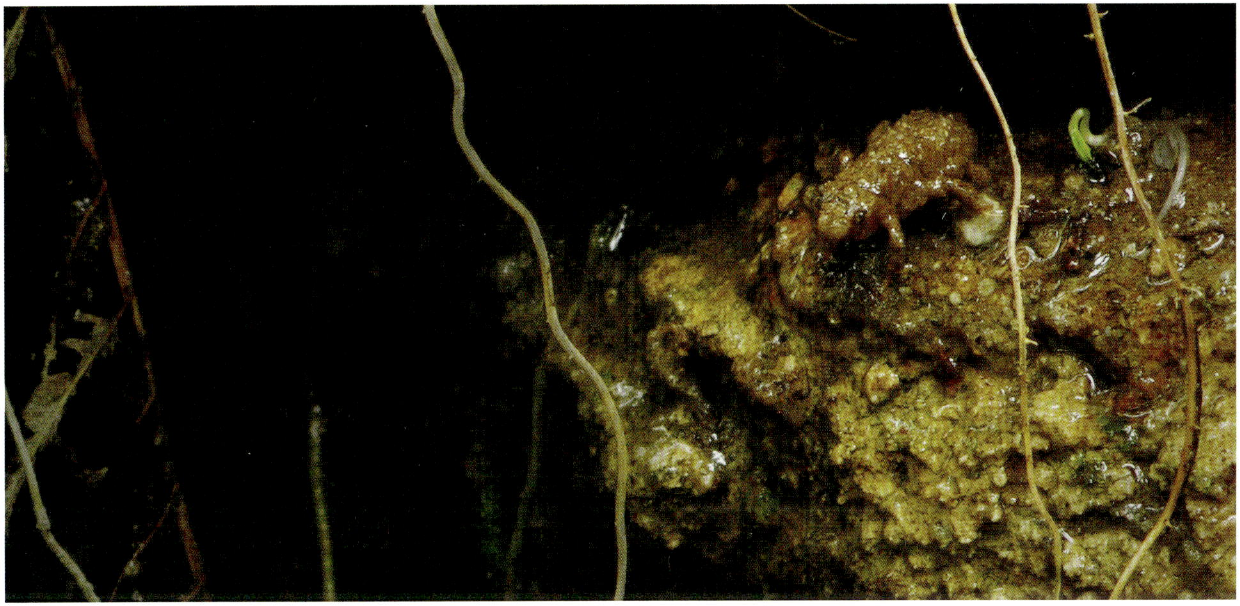

Larva of Tanypteryx pryeri / Larva of dragonfly (Early May, Kyushu)　ムカシヤンマの幼虫（5月初旬 鹿児島県）

Serene month
pale purple flowers
greet with tenderness

清和月　うすむらさきの
花やさし

Their rainbow colored wings always seduce me to take photos.
Today, let's make him pose on a bellflower. Their Japanese name is akagane-saruhamusi and 'saru' in Japanese (meaning 'monkey' in English) is said to derive from 'kukuri-zaru', or a monkey that cannot move with their arms and legs tied, and its round shape is considered good luck representing people's prayer for making their wishes come true by curbing other desires. Grape leaf beetle eat leaves of plants including leaf of crimson glory wine while their larvae eat roots of plants underground.

虹色の翅のこの虫を見つけると、いつもシャッターを押したくなります。
今日は、すぐ近くに咲いているキキョウソウに乗ってもらいましょう。名前の中の"サル"は"くくり猿"からきているそうです。お猿さんが手足をくくられて動けない姿を表した丸っこい縁起物で、欲望が動かないようにという願いがあるそうです。
ヤマブドウなどの葉を食べ、幼虫は地中で植物の根を食べるそうです。

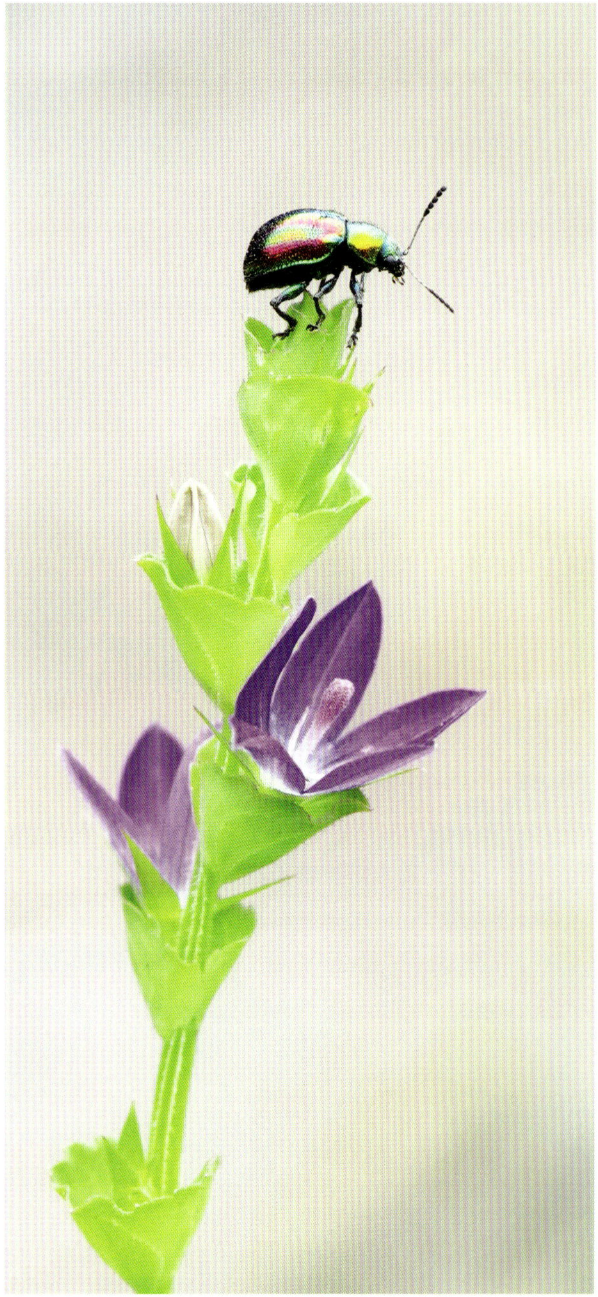

Acrothinium gaschkevitchii /
Grape leaf beetle (May, Kyushu)
アカガネサルハムシ（5月 鹿児島県）

Zephyr blows
legendary horse gallops through
in the far off sky

清風や　天馬遼空
駆けぬける

Walking in the forest searching for insects,
I nearly hit my head at a greenbrier tree which was generously putting its leaves.
Looking up, I found a pair of red leaf beetles clinging to its stem. The thorn's tendril looked like a leg of a horse flying in the sky. I pressed the shutter button against the sky. Leaf beetles, about 8 mm size, live across Japan from Hokkaido to Kyushu and can be found from spring to summer.
Both larva and imago eat leaves of greenbrier and smilax.

虫を探しながら林道を歩いているとき、のびのびと新芽を伸ばしたサルトリイバラに
頭がぶつかりそうになりました。見上げると、赤いハムシのペアがつかまっています。
イバラの巻きひげが空を飛ぶ馬の脚のようです。空をバックにシャッターを押します。
大きさ8ミリほど。北海道から九州にすんでいて、春から夏まで見られます。
幼虫も成虫もサルトリイバラやシオデの葉を食べるそうです。

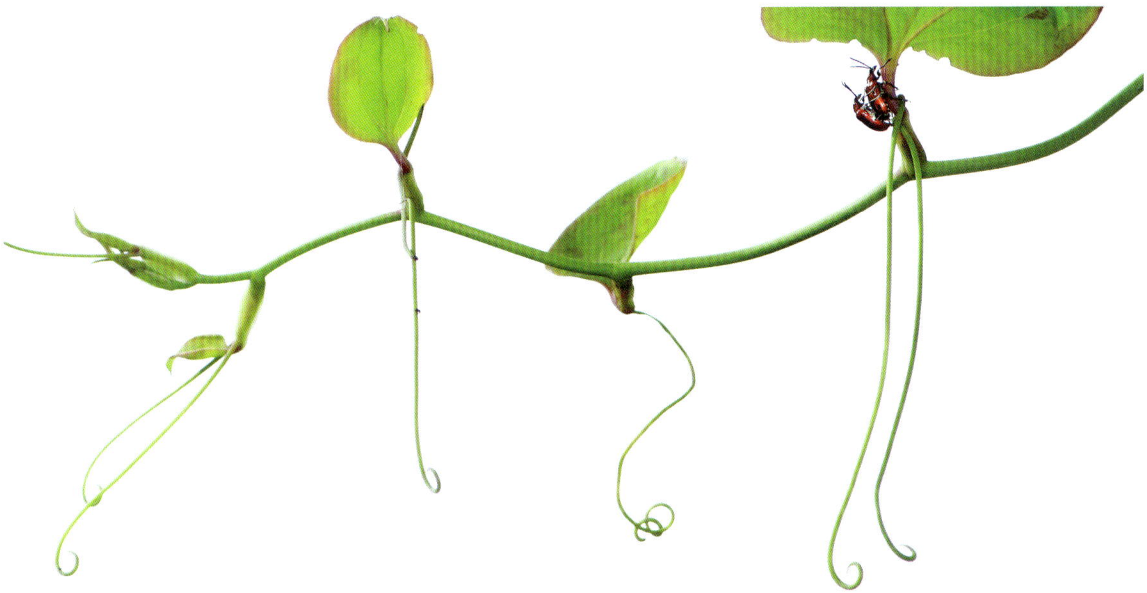

Liliocerís subpolita / Scarlet lily beetle (May, Kyushu)　アカクビナガハムシ（5月 鹿児島県）

High up in the sky
a bee draws a circle
preaching the course of life

九天に　○を描いて
道を説く

At a park which an insect lover friend of mine recommended, I saw horsetail bees here and there, putting their heads into holes in an oak tree and checking inside. They were looking for larvae of long-horned beetle hiding in the trunk in order to lay eggs on them. A horsetail bee began to take care of her ovipositor, seven times larger than herself, by stroking skillfully with her hind legs. Looking at the tips of the hind legs, we can find the ovipositor consisting from three pipes. They live in the main island and Kyushu region.

虫友に教わった公園では、コナラの木に開いている穴に頭をつっこんで、中を点検している姿があちこちで見られました。木の幹に潜んでいるシロスジカミキリの幼虫を探して卵を産みつけるのだそうです。1頭が葉の上で、体長の7倍以上もある産卵管の手入れを始めました。後脚で上手にしごきます。脚の先を見ると、産卵管が3本からできていることがわかります。本州から九州にすんでいます。

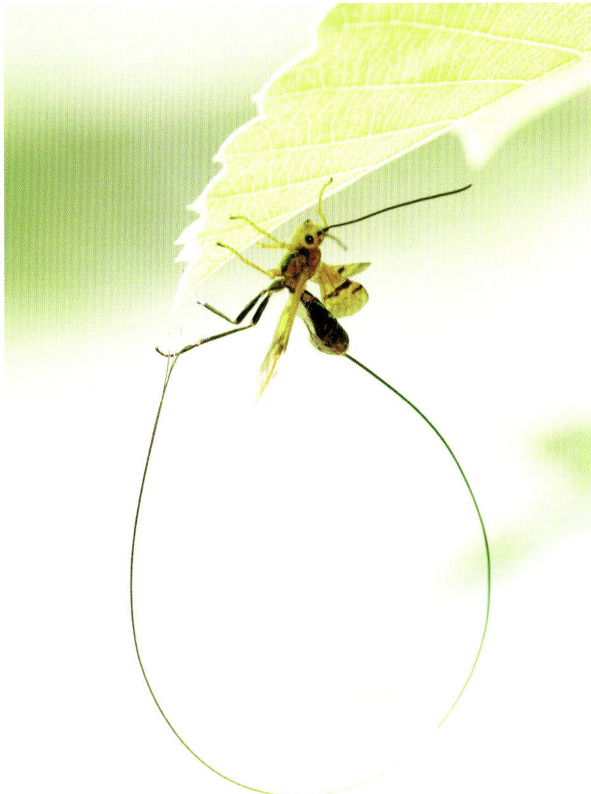

Euurobracon yokohamae /
Horsetail bee (May, Kyushu)
ウマノオバチ（5月 鹿児島県）

Pure white blossoms and fresh smelling young leaves wrap a path in the field

花しろく　匂う若葉の
野のこみち

I feel really good to walk on a mountain path on a fine day of the season of fresh green.
The air is filled with the fragrance of hydrangea, and horseflies along with long-horned beetles are indulged in their delicacies. Larvae of Japanese broad-winged katydid are no exception.
I saw many larvae sitting on hydrangea. They seem to like the flower.
It seems to me that grasshoppers look prettier when larva than imago, but what do you think?
They came from southern hemisphere and they live around the main island to Okinawa islands.

天気のいい若葉の季節に山道を歩くのは、ほんとうに気持ちがいいです。
あちこちに咲いているガクウツギの花が匂って、アブやカミキリたちがごちそうに夢中です。
クダマキモドキの幼虫もこの花が好きなようで、白い花に乗っているのをたくさん見かけました。
バッタのなかまは成虫よりも幼虫の方がかわいいと思いますがいかがでしょう。
南方系の虫で、本州から沖縄にすんでいます。

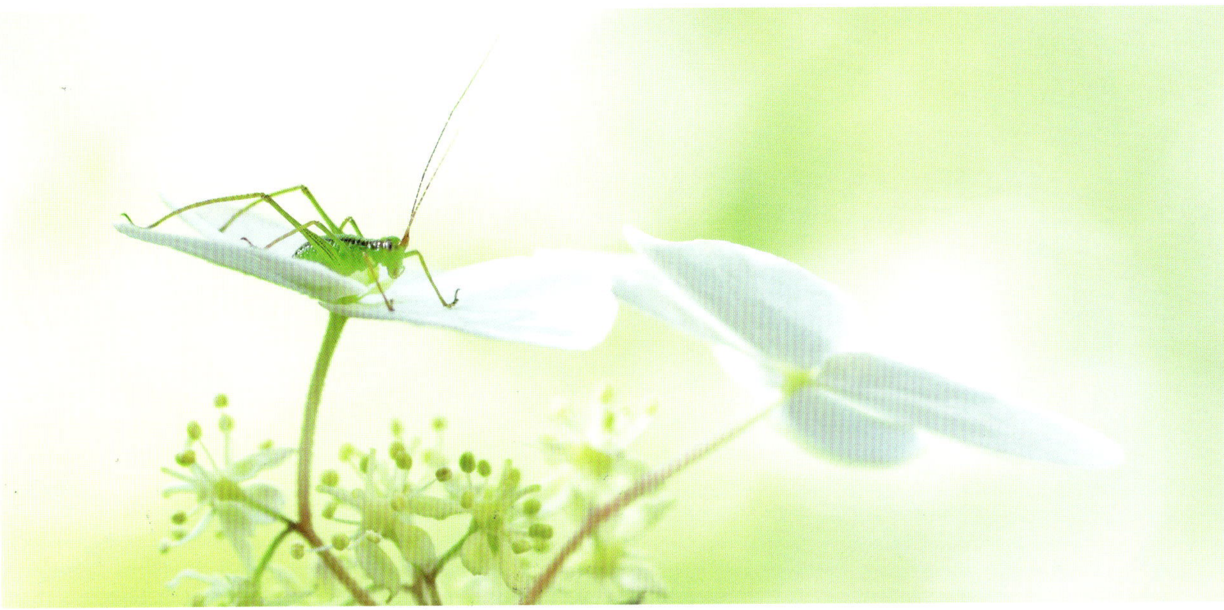

Larva of Holochlora japonica / Larva of Japanese broad-winged katydid (May, Kyushu)　クダマキモドキの一種の幼虫(5月 鹿児島県)

Spring to Summer

春から夏へ

People prepare the planting of rice seedlings in paddies.

水田では田植えの準備が
始まります

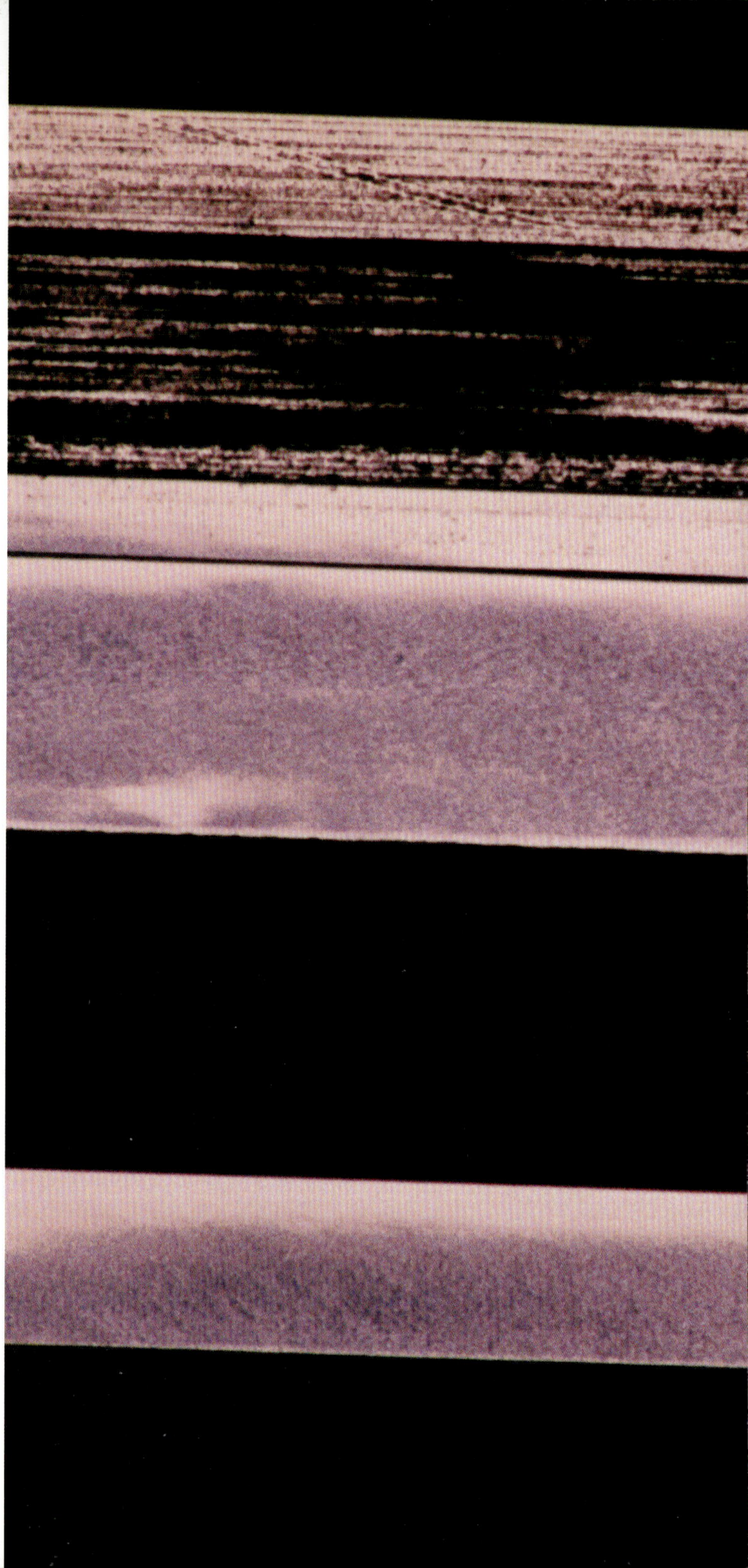

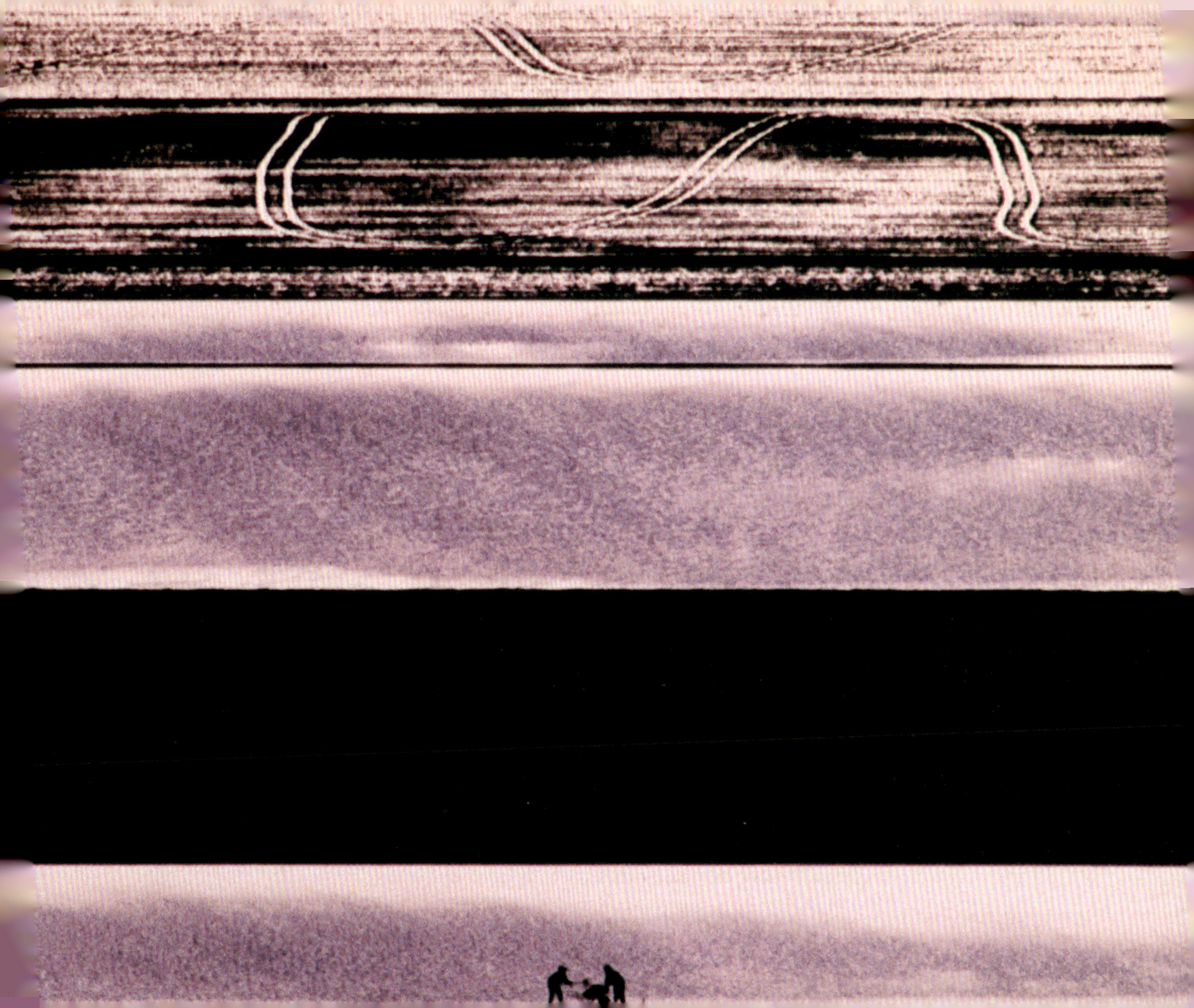

Sumo match between insects
exchanging slapping
repeating hakkeyoi

虫ずもう　張り手のおうしゅう
ハッケヨイ

On a verdant leaf in the sunshine, males were having Sumo wrestling match.
They were looking strong with muscles of thighs and arms. Perhaps they were fighting for a female.
Female makes cradle for eggs by rolling leaves of sawtooth oak or rose.
Black leaf-rolling weevils in Kansai and westward regions have yellow-brown legs and abdomen,
those in Kanto region are black all over while those in Tohoku region have red wings.
Their body length is about 5mm and they are seen from spring to summer.

お日様いっぱいの新緑の葉の上で、オスたちが相撲をとっています。
太ももや腕の筋肉が盛り上がっていて強そうです。近くにいるメスのとりあいなのでしょうか？
メスはクヌギやバラなどの葉を巻いて卵の入ったゆりかごを作ります。
近畿以西は脚と腹部が黄褐色、関東付近は全身黒色、東北にすんでいるものは
翅が赤いそうです。大きさ5ミリほどで春から夏にかけて見られます。

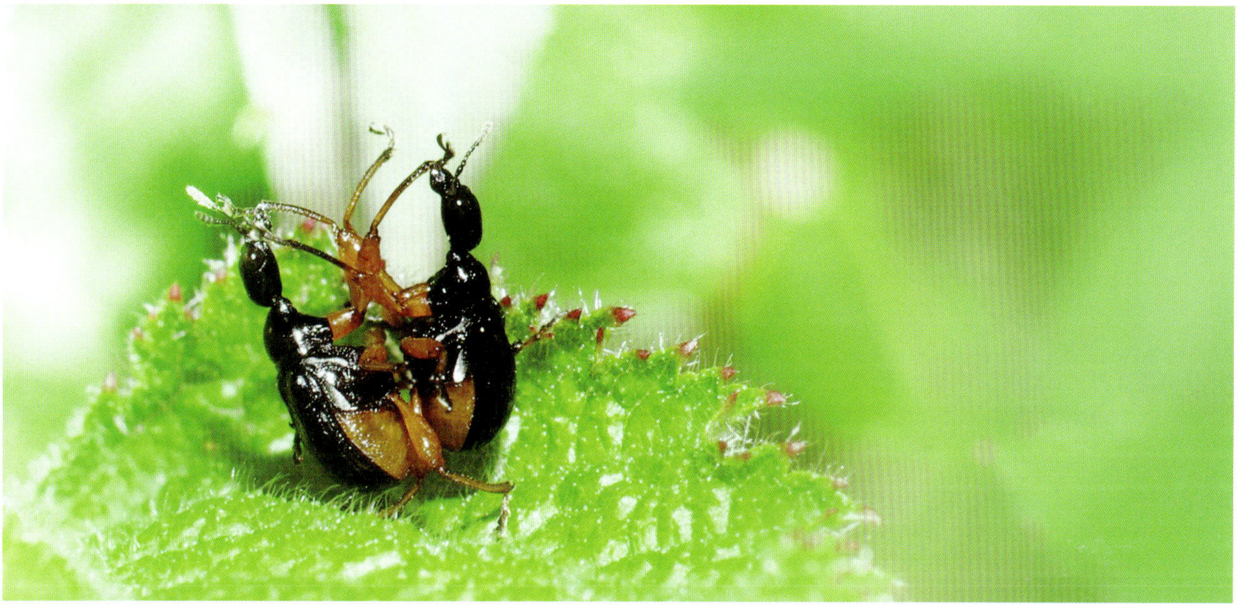

Apoderus erythrogaster / Black leaf-rolling weevil (April, Kyushu)　ヒメクロオトシブミ(4月 鹿児島県)

In a summer shade rests a cool guy in yukata

夏陰に　ゆかた姿の
クールガイ

Hogweeds were blossoming along waterways over which many fireflies would fly in a week.
Butterflies avidly sucking honey from the umbrella-like white flowers do not mind anyone passing by.
The honey must be delicious. I released the shutter waiting the butterfly to rest on a spot where
I could have a good contrast with the flowers. Characterized by the stone-wall pattern on their wings,
this species of butterfly rests on flowers or plants with its wings opened.
They live in the main island through Okinawa islands and their larva eats leaves of ficus.

1週間後にはたくさんのホタルが飛び交う水路の縁にハナウドが咲いています。
チョウは傘のような白い花の蜜を吸うのに夢中で、近くを人が通っても気にしません。
よほどおいしい蜜なのでしょう。花に同化しない場所に来るのを待ってシャッターを切ります。
特徴的な石垣模様をしたチョウで、ほとんど翅を開いてとまります。
本州から沖縄にすんでいて幼虫はイヌビワやオオイタビを食べます。

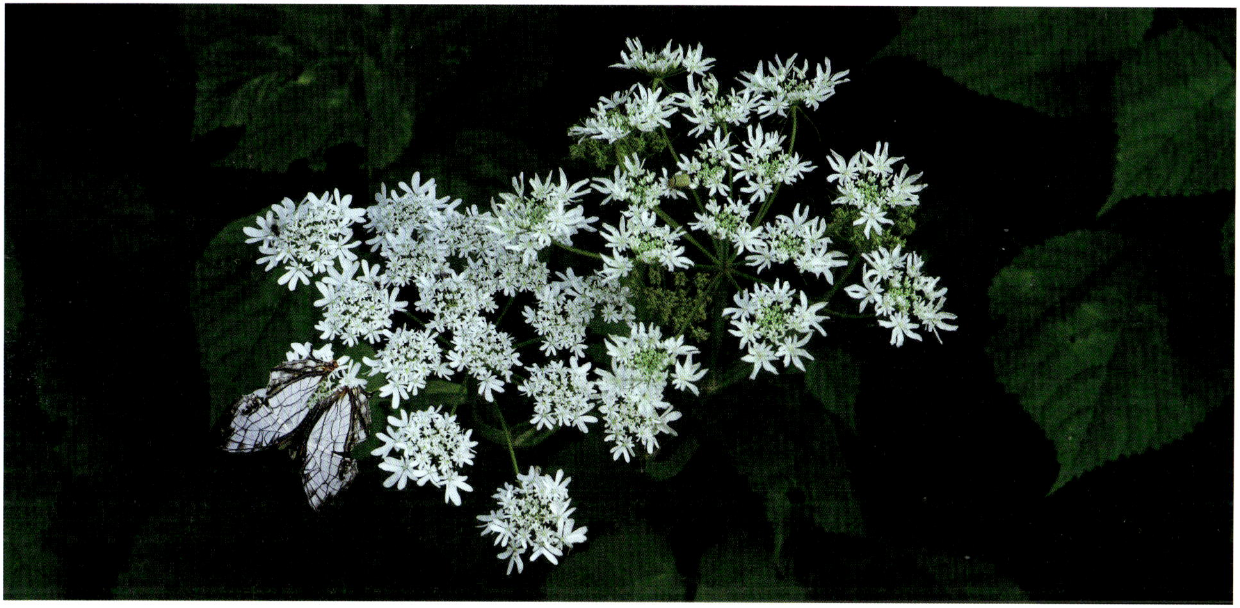

Cyrestis thyodamas / Nymphalid butterfly (May, Kyushu)　イシガケチョウ（5月 鹿児島県）

Under sun shower
though how short it may be
a new life is born

白雨きて　細きいのちの
生まれけり

A friend of mine made ponds around his house and enjoys lotuses and water lilies. There are several small ponds where lots of dragonflies live. I found a newly emerged damselfly at one of his ponds after a sudden rain. Damselflies can be categorized into two types: little damselfly which emerges early summer and live until autumn, and slightly bigger damselfly which emerges in autumn and live through the winter. The one I saw seems to be the former. This species is endemic to Japan and lives from the main island to Kyushu.

家の周りに池を作って、蓮や睡蓮などを楽しんでいる友人がいます。小さな池がいくつかあって、トンボもたくさんすんでいます。突然の大粒の雨が上がったあと、羽化したばかりのホソミイトトンボを見つけました。初夏に羽化して秋まで見られるやや小さい夏型と、少し後に羽化して越冬する少し大きい越冬型があるそうです。これは夏型かな。日本特産種で本州から九州にすんでいます。

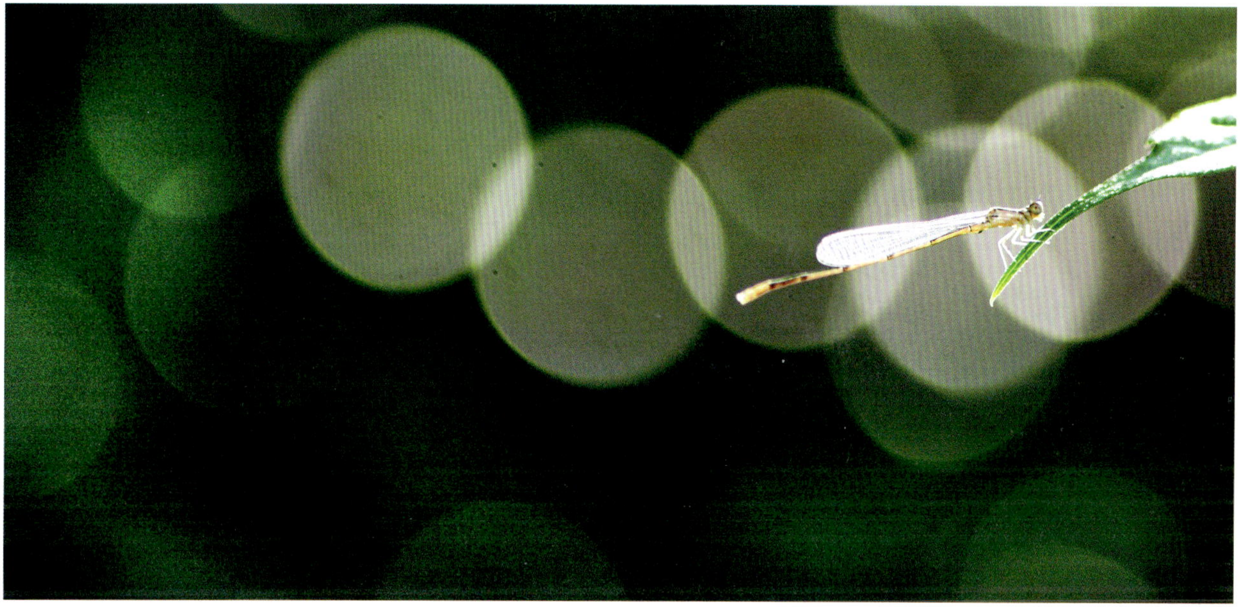

Aciagrion migratum / Damselfly (June, Kyushu)　ホソミイトトンボ（6月 鹿児島県）

In a shade of young leaf
he stands high
with self-reliance and self-respect

青葉陰　自立自尊の
虫ありき

Good-looking with long antennae, fairy longhorn moth is one of my favorite moths.
I came across him flying faintly when walking on a dim path of forest, but this type of moth can often be seen in sunny places as well. They fly clumsily as if they don't know what to do with their antennae.
Their body length is about 8 mm and male's antennae are as long as 25 mm,
whereas female's antennae are shorter and its half part is covered with black hair.
You can see this species from spring to summer.

触角が長くてかっこいい、大好きな蛾のひとつです。
これは木の葉のおおいかぶさった暗い林道を歩いていて、ちらちらと飛んでいるところを見つけました。陽のあたるところにも多く、触角をもてあますように不器用に飛びます。
体長8ミリほどですが、オスの触角は25ミリ程もあります。メスの触角はずっと短くて、根元から半分が黒い毛で覆われています。春から夏にかけて見られます。

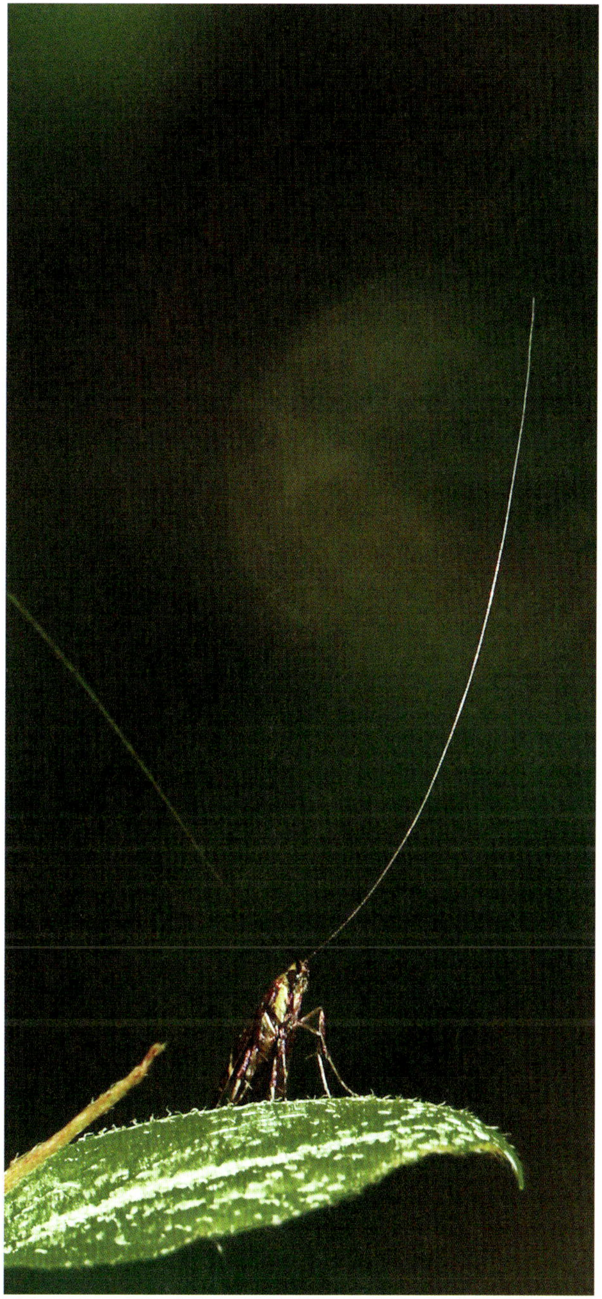

Nemophora aurifera /
Fairy longhorn moth (May, Kyushu)
ホソオビヒゲナガ(5月 鹿児島県)

In a morning of fog
a tiny life is saved
let it live in today

霧の朝　今日もいちにち
生かされる

A dense fog blanketed a village near river with lot of dews falling on weeds.
When I was walking around looking for insects, I saw a grass blue butterfly flying from somewhere and rest on a leaf. Stay there, stay! Lying on the ground I focused the lens on the butterfly and luckily the sun started to appear behind him. Their japanese name 'yamato' means 'Japan' in English, which shows this species is a very common insect that can be seen from early spring to late autumn.
Their body length is about 12 mm. Their larvae grow feeding on sorrels.

川に近い村は濃い霧がたちこめていて、まわりの草には露がいっぱい。
何かいないかなあと見まわしていると、どこからかシジミチョウが飛んできて葉の上にとまりました。
そのままそのまま！　腹ばいになってレンズを向けると、ちょうど奥から陽が昇ってきました。
ヤマトの名のとおり、春先から秋遅くまで普通に見られます。大きさ12ミリほど。
幼虫はカタバミを食べて成長します。

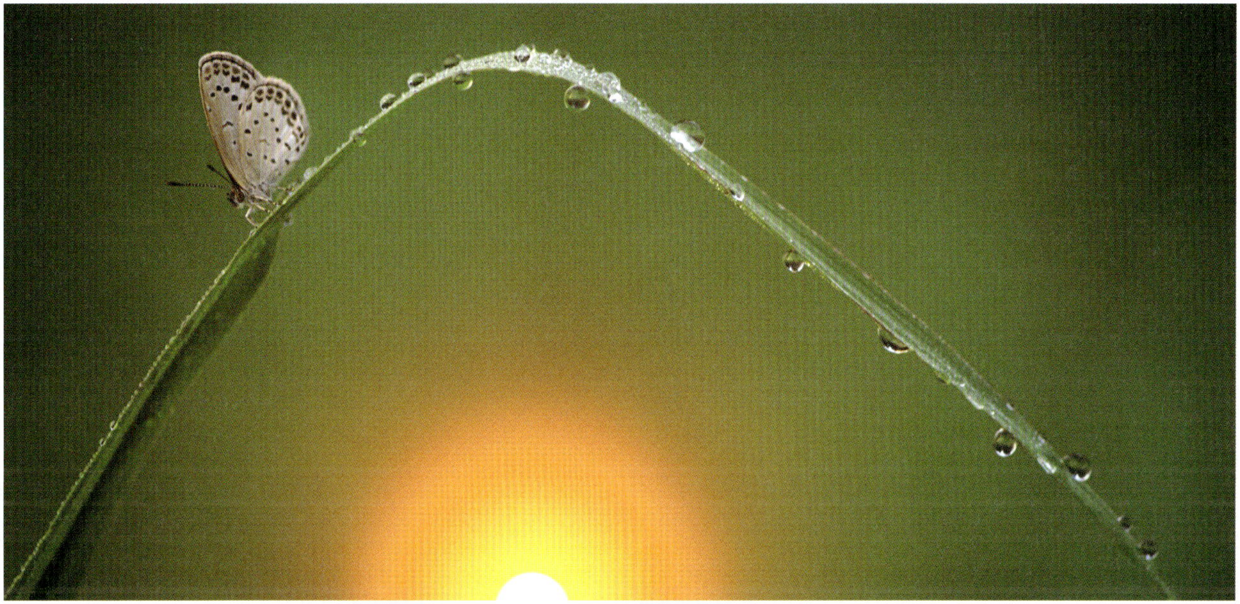

Pseudozizeeria maha / Grass blue butterfly (May, Kyushu)　ヤマトシジミ（5月 鹿児島県）

Let's take one step toward the firmament on this fine day of rainy season

梅雨晴れや　ステップはるか 天空へ

Five insect lover fellows including me, one day, introduced fields respectively.
Each of us has that kind of secret fields and we enjoyed taking photos of insects all day long.
I found a tiny ladybird in the meadow. Lying on the grass, I released the shutter toward the sky.
I am not sure if the ladybird is a Phymatosternus lewisii. I cannot identify because this photo
is the only one I have. Their size is about 4 mm and they live from the main island to Kyushu region.
Both larva and imago feed on aphids.

虫仲間5人で、おたがいの得意のフィールドをまわりながら、
1日中虫の写真を撮って遊んだことがあります。案内された草原で
小さなテントウムシを見つけました。草の下にねころんで、空に向けてシャッターを押します。
多分ヨツボシテントウかなあ？ 写真だけなので同定*3には自信がありません。大きさ4ミリくらい。
本州から九州にかけてすんでいて、幼虫も成虫もアブラムシを食べます。

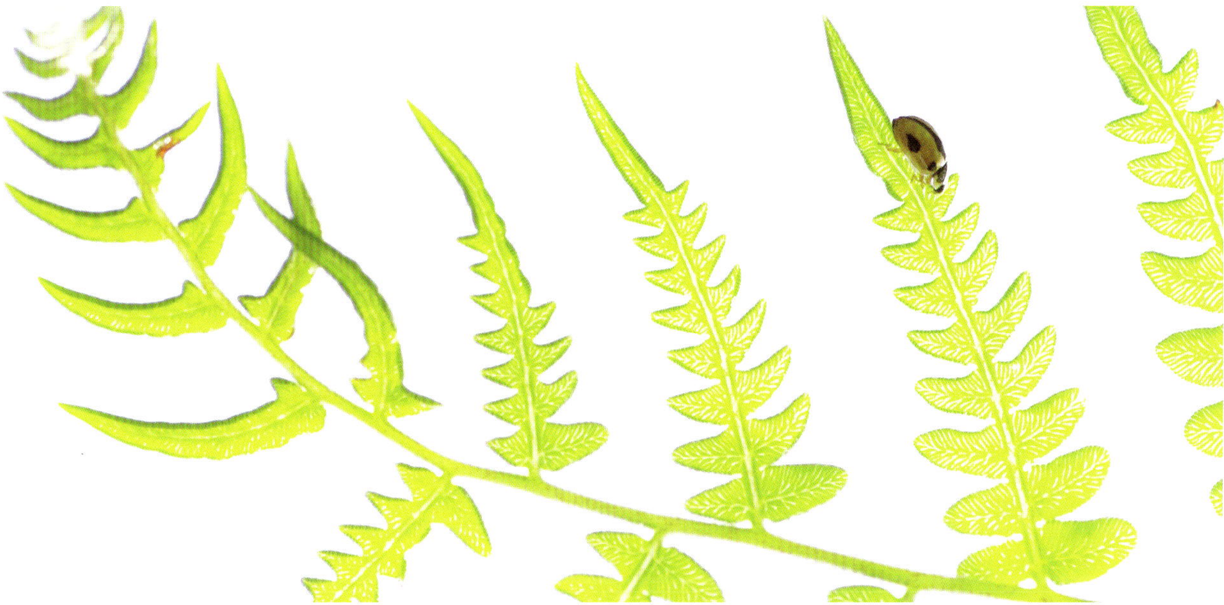

Phymatosternus lewisii / Ladybird (June, Kyushu)　ヨツボシテントウ（6月 鹿児島県）

In a doze
nothing is heard
but river and cicadas

まどろめば　ただ川の音
せみの声

Males were patiently waiting for female on small stones here and there, claiming their territories. Females come to attach eggs there. I was looking attentively at the stream like male gomphidae, but a gentle river breeze tempted me to fall into a doze. Early summer is the season where we can find opportunities to take shots of two species at a time. Calopteryx cornelia emerges in early summer and Mnais pruinosa in spring. They are both endemic to Japan.

あちこちの小石の上で、オジロサナエのオスが産卵にくるメスをしんぼう強く待っています。産卵を撮ろうと、オスと同じくじっと眼をこらしていた私も、心地よい川風に誘われて眠たくなってきました。小川の石の上ではカワトンボたちが縄張りを張っています。ミヤマカワトンボが出始める初夏、春に羽化するアサヒナカワトンボとの2ショットを撮る機会があります。両種とも日本特産種です。

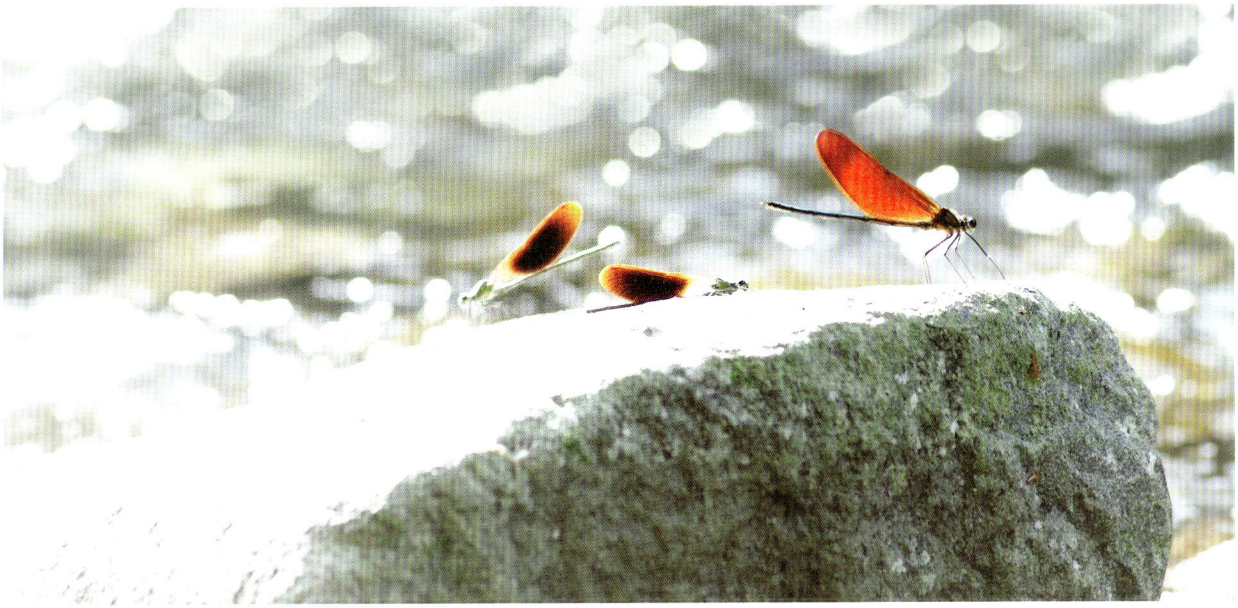

Mnais pruinosa & Calopteryx cornelia / Large damselfly (June, Kyushu)　アサヒナカワトンボとミヤマカワトンボ（6月 鹿児島県）

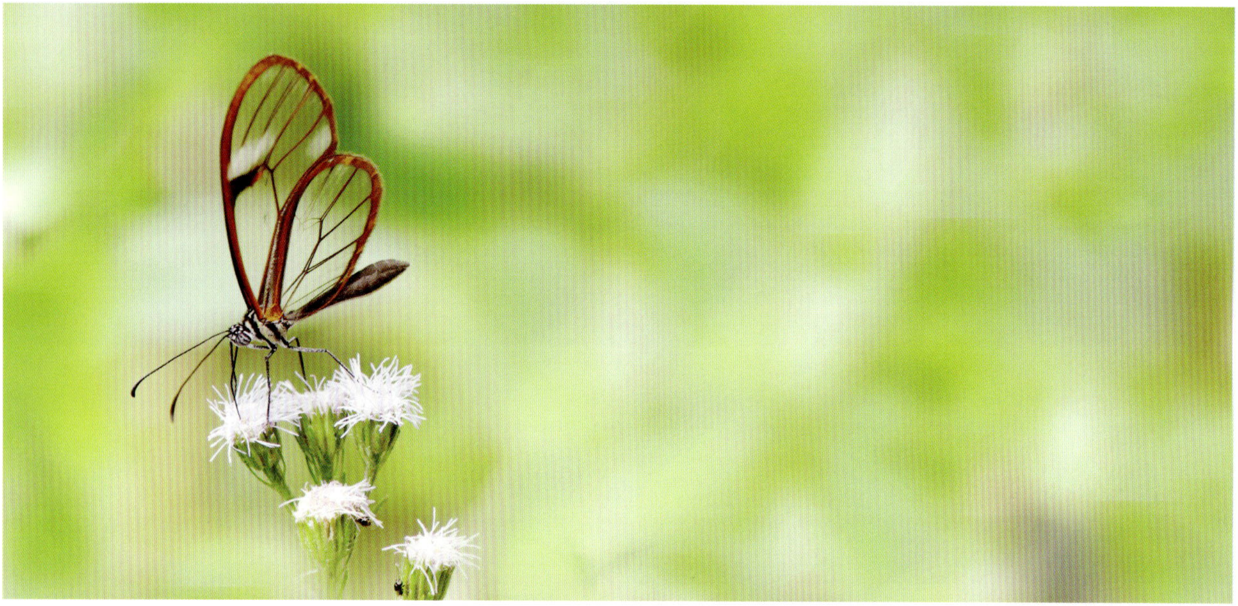

Hypoleria sp. / Glasswing butterfly (July, Monteverde / Costa Rica)　トンボマダラ（スカシマダラ）の一種（7月 モンテベルデ／コスタリカ）

Through wing of glass a whole universe appears
in front of you

身を透かし　生きれば宇宙が
見えてくる

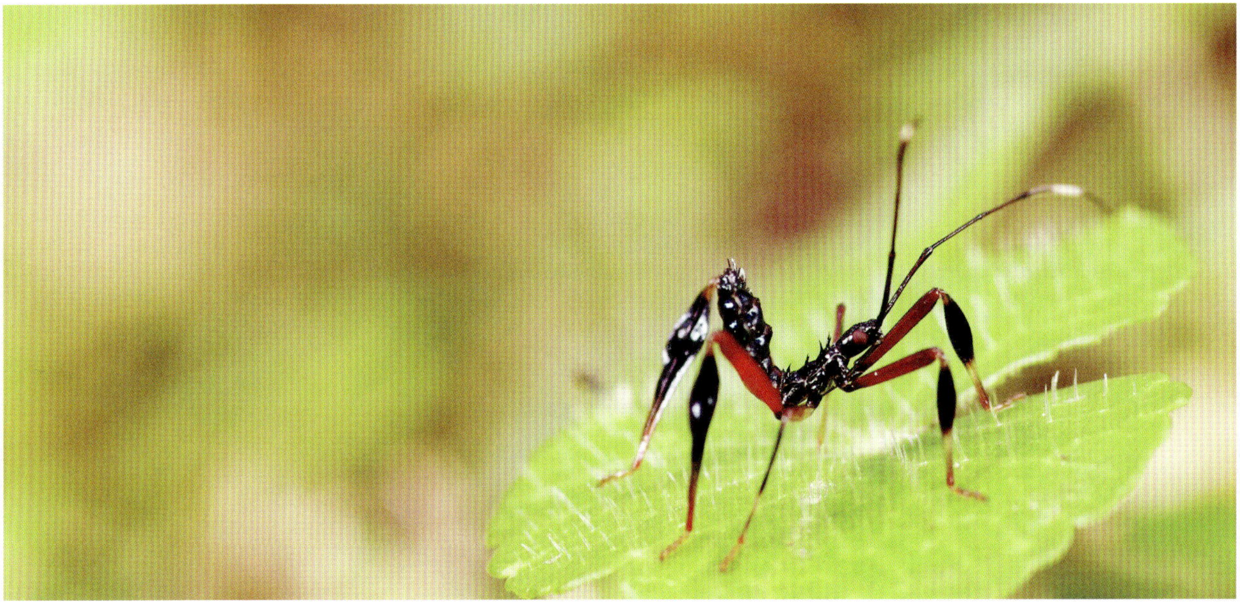

Larva of Reduviidae sp. / Larva of Assassin bug (July, Monteverde / Costa Rica)　サシガメの一種の幼虫（7月 モンテベルデ／コスタリカ）

Tiny little robot living in a tropic land
peaceful and tranquil

熱帯の　ミニミニロボット
ゆるゆるり

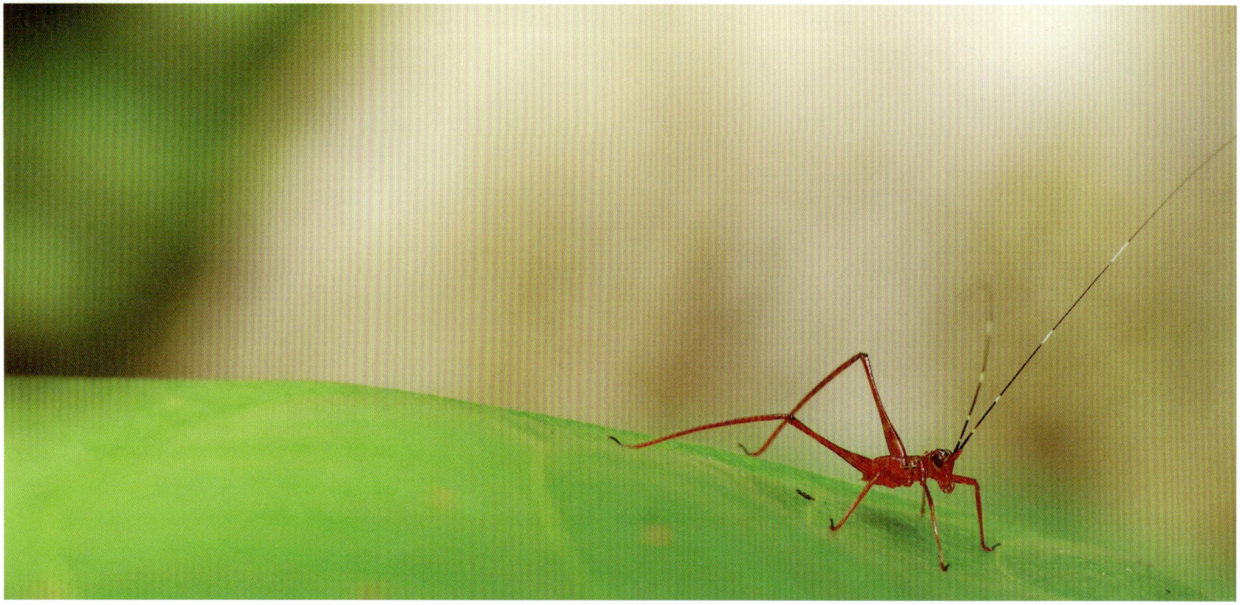

Larva of Gampsocleis sp. / Larva of grasshopper (July, Bacan / Indonesia)　キリギリスの一種の幼虫（7月 バチャン島／インドネシア）

What a joy to play with the child of the Sun
at the equator

赤道で　太陽の子と
遊びけり

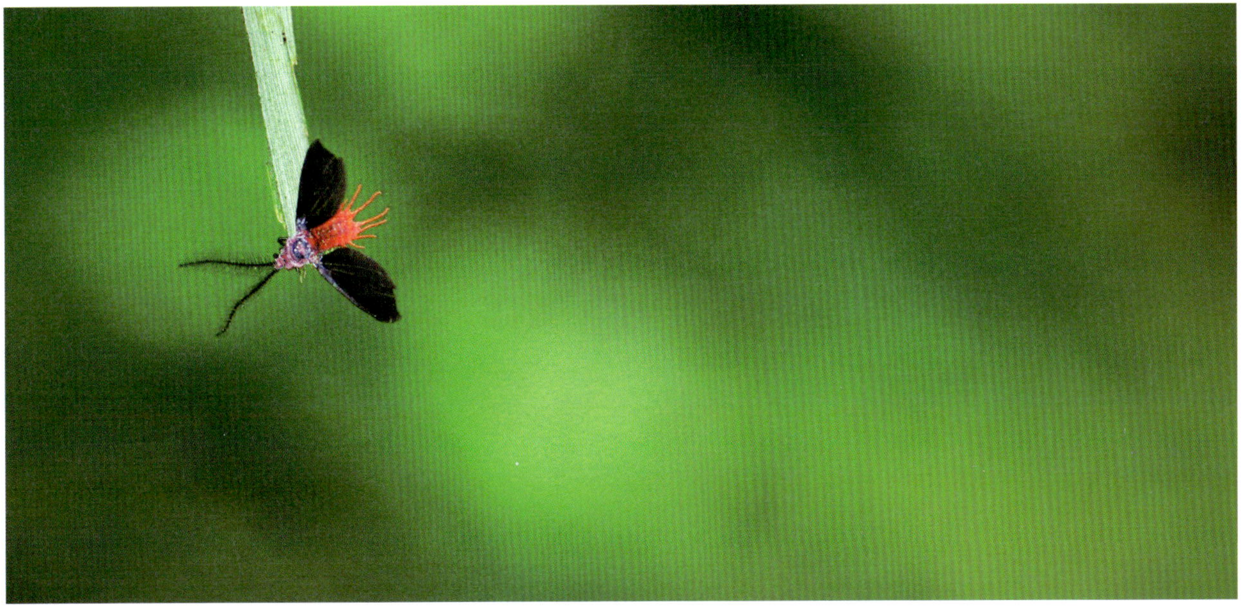

Male coccoidea sp. / Male mealybug (July, Bacan / Indonesia)　カイガラムシの一種の雄（7月 バチャン島／インドネシア）

In the wood shade
a loving Tinker Bell is capering

木下闇　ティンカーベルが
舞っており

Flower float parades with a little escort dressed in tea green

花車　御伴は緑の
京衣

Magnolias were blossoming along the mountain path. Some in buds,
some just started to bloom and some faded. Among flowers, I found a shiny green beetle.
I often come across them when walking in the mountains in summer.
Their beauty fascinates me so much that I cannot help but release the shutter button.
Their body size is about 10 mm and they live in south of the main island.
Larvae eat dead trees and imagoes suck nectar.

山路にオオヤマレンゲが咲いています。
蕾のもの、咲き始めのもの、咲き終わったもの。盛りを過ぎた花の中に、
金緑色の甲虫を見つけました。夏の山を歩いているとあちこちで見かけますが、
きれいなので会うたびにシャッターを押すことになります。本州以南にすんでいて、
大きさ10ミリほど。幼虫は枯れ木を食べ、成虫は花の蜜を吸うそうです。

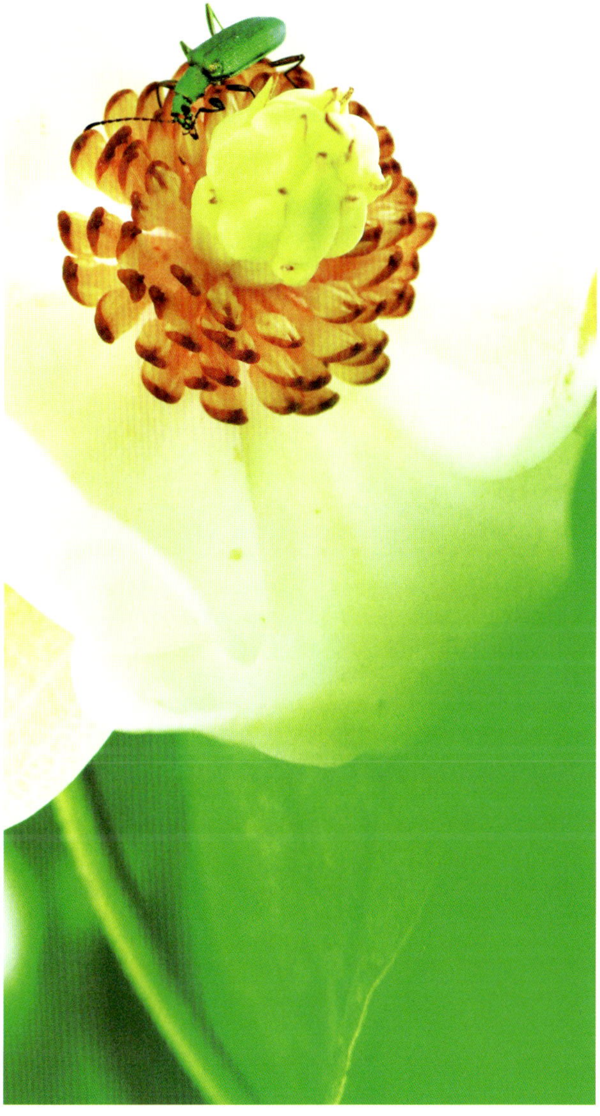

Arthromacra decora /
Long-joined beetle (July, Gifu)
アオハムシダマシ(7月 岐阜県)

Still water of the island takes me far away from the world

美ら島の　清き流れに世を忘れ

Guided by one of my insect lover friends,
I came to a miraculous place where river flowed so still after climbing up a steep slope.
The stream was crystal clear, above which many damselflies were flying with their glittering pale blue wings.
We decided to stay all day. With the distinct stigma on their wings, female usually lay eggs on
decayed wood in the stream and they are often seen dive into water. Broad-winged damselflies live in
Amami Oshima and Okinawa islands and we can see them there almost throughout the year.

急な斜面の踏み跡を奥へ進むと、奇蹟のように平らな川原が現れました。
流れる水は切れるように清らかで、たくさんのトンボが明るい縹色[*4]の翅表をきらきら
輝かせて飛んでいます。今日は1日、案内してくれた虫友とここで遊びましょう。
黒い翅に白い縁紋が目立つメスは、川の中の朽ち木に産卵することが多く、
しばしば水中に潜ります。奄美大島と沖縄にすんでいて、ほとんど年中見られます。

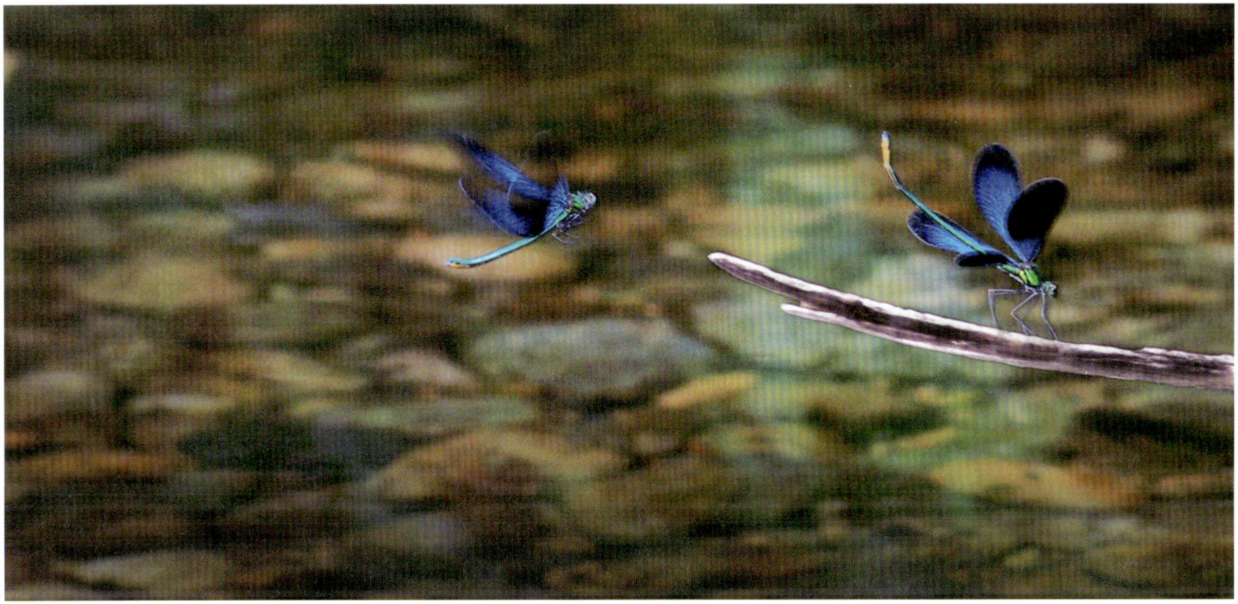

Matrona basilaris / Broad-winged damselfly (August, Amami Oshima Island / Kyushu)　リュウキュウハグロトンボ(8月 奄美大島)

Surrendered to the wind flying high from the heat of lazy afternoon

日盛りを　はるかな風に
ゆだねけり

The director of aquatic garden created a pond in a rice field and I found many flutterers flying that day.
They looked flying without any purpose, but they were actually waiting for females which sometimes come there to attach eggs. Blue-shining wide wings are the signature of the species.
The color of wings changes slightly depending on the angles from which you see.
Flutterers tell us the beginning of summer. We sense autumn in the air when they are getting less.
They live from the main island through Kyushu.

水生植物園の園長が、たんぼに水を張って池を作ってくれました。
今日はチョウトンボがいっぱい。悠々と飛んでいるようですが、
たまに産卵にやってくるメスを捕まえようと見張っているのです。幅の広い青く輝く翅が
トレードマーク。翅の色は見る角度によって微妙に変わります。このトンボが出てくると夏の始まり。
少なくなると秋の気配が漂います。本州から九州にすんでいます。

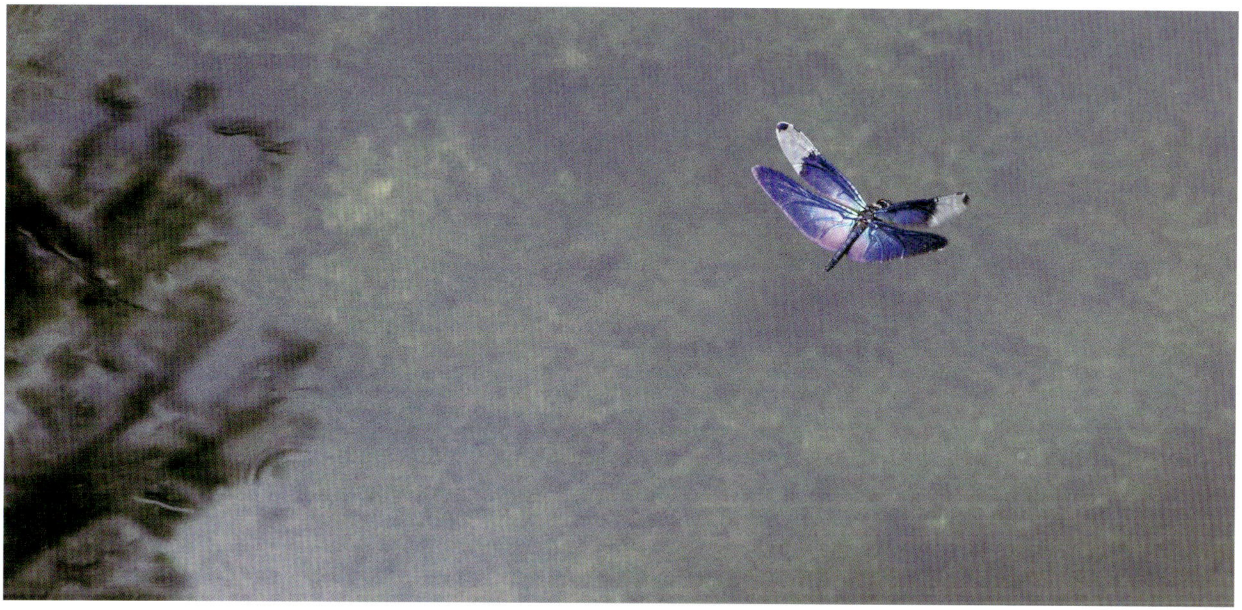

Rhyothemis fuliginosa / Flutterer (August, Kyushu)　チョウトンボ(8月 鹿児島県)

Harvest moon hidden
behind clouds of silk curtain
mountain chill fill the air

名月を　かくして山の
冷気かな

The insect lover friend of mine always has everything he needs for insect-watching in his car; white cloth, generator, fluorescent lamp and so on. We were supposed to enjoy harvest moon that night but thick clouds covered the sky and drizzle was falling occasionally. Spreading white cloth with light on, we waited for insects to come. It was past eight o'clock when a large moth appeared with rustling sound. Moths overturn very often being unable to manage their wings. I took a shot after waiting for him to rest on a branch. Larva is said to eat leaves of fagaceae plants.

虫友の車には、白布、発電機、蛍光灯など、全部積んであります。今日は満月のはずですが、厚い雲におおわれ、ときに霧雨も降る冷たい夜です。白布を張って電気を灯し、虫が来るのを待ちます。夜8時を過ぎた頃、ばさばさと大きな蛾がやってきました。翅をもてあまして、地面の上でよくひっくり返ります。木枝にとまってもらって写真を撮りました。幼虫はブナ科の植物の葉を食べるそうです。

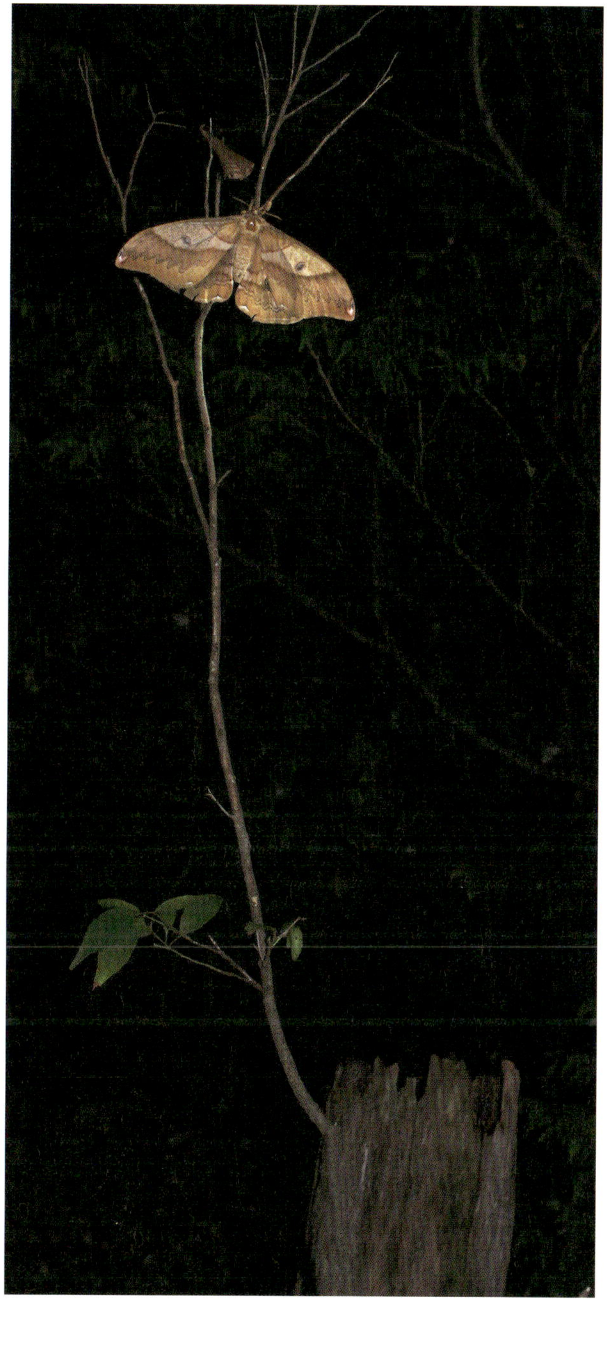

Antheraea yamamai /
Japanese silk moth
(September, Kyushu)
ヤママユガ(9月 鹿児島県)

Deep into the mountain where the stream shimmers a one-man-show begins

奥山の　川でひとりの
夏舞台

With rice balls and water canteen, I often spend hot summer days in a stream.
Broad-winged damselfly with reddish brown wings and purple-copper-colored tail is one of my favorite insects and they often do a headstand under the summer sun. It is said they do headstand because they want to keep their body away from the sun as much as possible. But you'll never know unless they tell you the truth.
Damselflies close their wings when they rest but open them suddenly from time to time. I released the shutter at this very moment. They are endemic to Japan and can be seen from June to September.

おにぎりと水筒を持って、暑い1日を川で遊びます。
赤褐色の翅と紫銅色の尾を持つ大好きなこのカワトンボは、日差しが強いとよく逆立ちをします。
陽のあたる面積を小さくするためという説もありますが、本当のところは
トンボにきかないとわかりません。とまると翅を閉じますが、ときどきぱっと開くので、
その瞬間にシャッターを切ります。6月から9月ごろまで見られます。日本特産種。

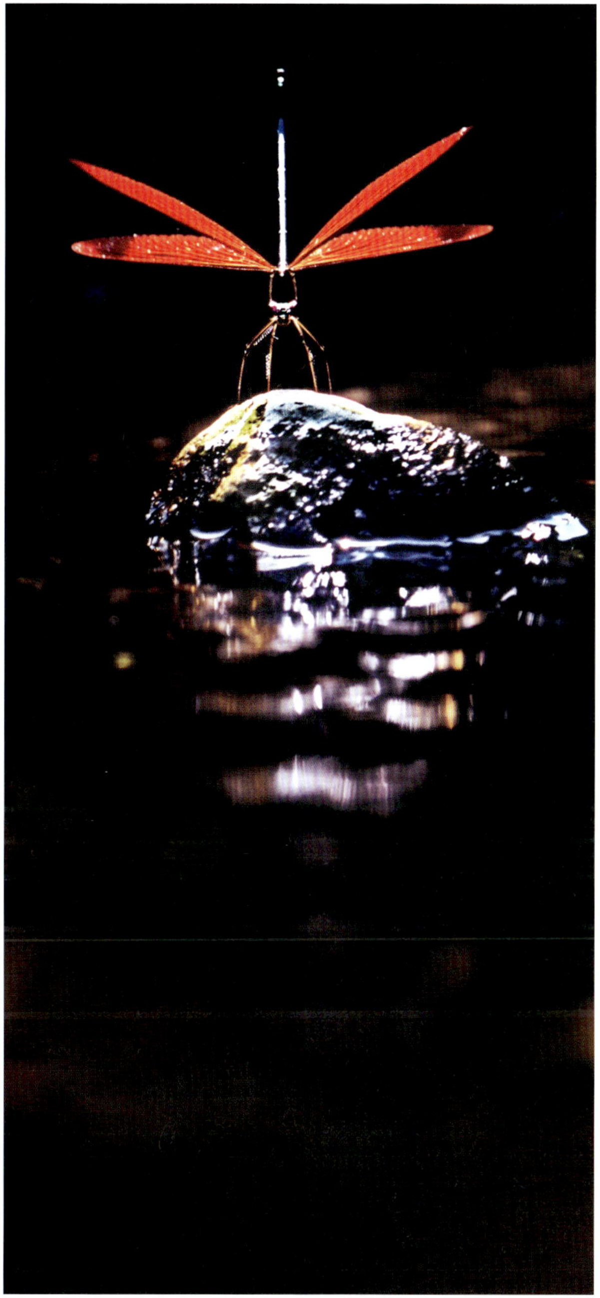

Calopteryx cornelia /
Broad-winged damselfly
(August, Kyushu)
ミヤマカワトンボ(8月 鹿児島県)

Summer to Autumn

夏から秋へ

The shadow of reeds stretches under the moonlight.

月はアシの影を長く伸ばします

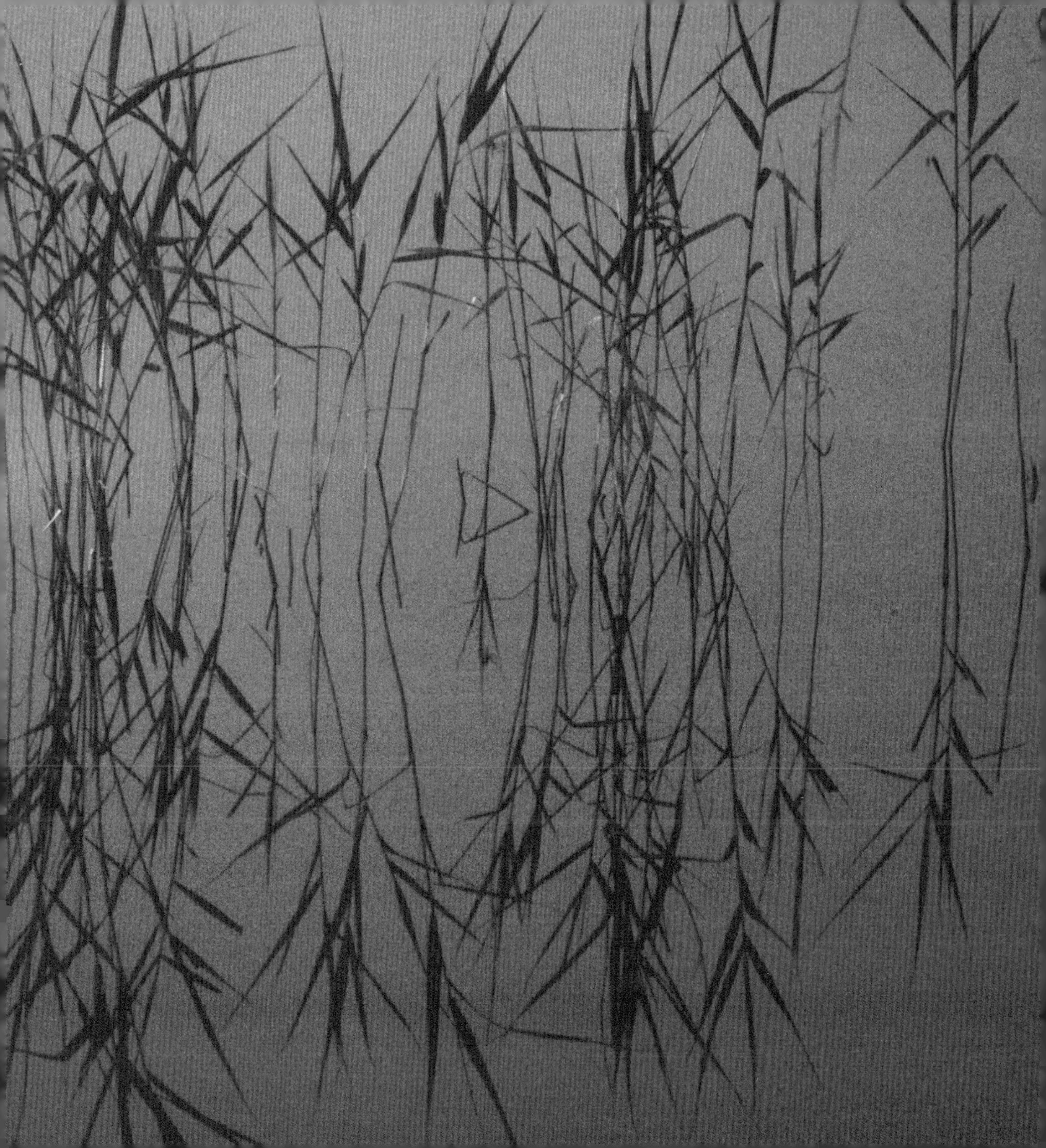

In the summer shade
radiates what tengu left
a small jade stone

夏陰や　天狗忘れた
翡翠だま

I found a jade-green gem on silver grass when I was climbing up a slope along mountain stream. The gem looked transparent under the afternoon sunshine. From the jade-like chrysalis emerge a blackish butterfly of about 35 mm in size. They are not interested in flowers and rest directly on the ground after flying fluffily above the forest floor. Larvae have black head and pale green abdomen and they are often seen on silver grass and coix plant. Dark Evening Brown live from the main island to Kyushu. Slightly bigger-sized type appears in autumn.

渓流沿いの坂を上っているとき、路の脇のススキで翡翠色の宝石を見つけました。
午後の陽に照らされて透けて見えます。この蛹から35ミリ程もある黒っぽいチョウが産まれます。
チョウは花には興味がなく、林床をふわふわと飛んで地面にとまります。
幼虫は黒い頭と薄緑色の胴体で、ススキやジュズダマでよく見つかります。
本州から九州にすんでいて、秋には少し大きな個体が出現します。

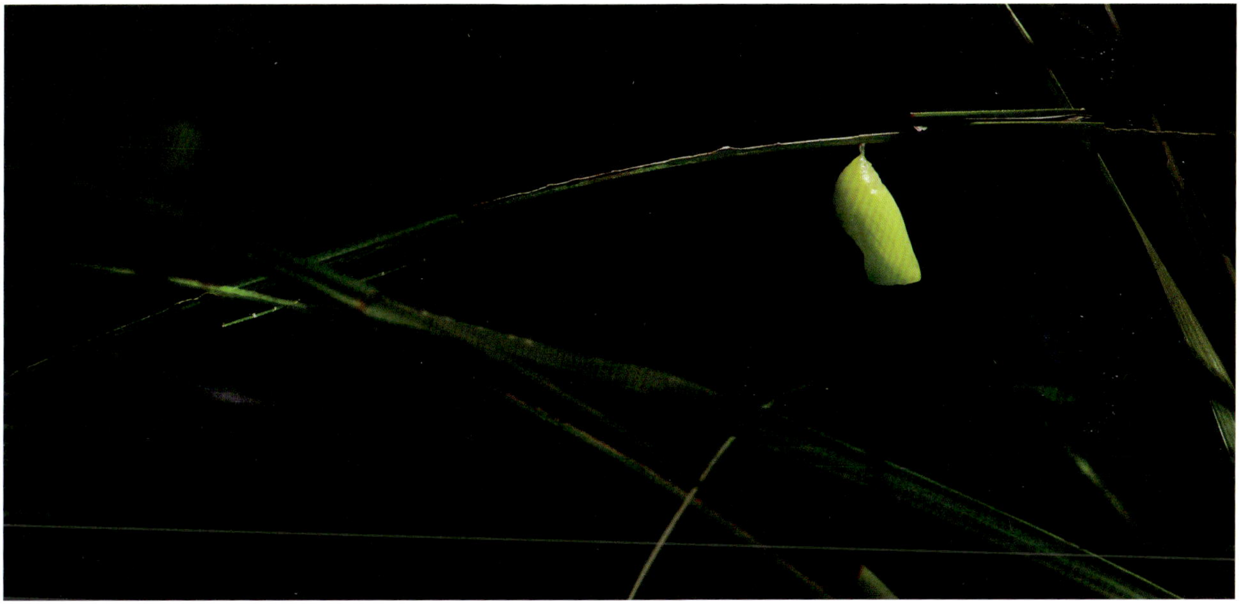

Chrysalis of Melanitis phedima / Chrysalis of Dark Evening Brown (July, Kyushu)　クロコノマチョウの蛹(7月 鹿児島県)

Twilight of Kannazuki
all the lights around them
start fading sweet and low

なかよしに　闇迫りけり
神無月

I was searching for insects all day long on an autumn day and this beautiful day drew to a close turning slowly to twilight. I saw something white glittering in the shadow when walking down a slope for home. I took a step closer and found two butterflies resting side by side like close friends on an ear tip of a crabgrass. They showed no sign of flying off from the tip even when it swayed in the wind as if they had decided to spend the whole night together. The body length of grass blue butterfly is about 12 mm. Larvae feed on creeping woodsorrel and are commonly seen near houses.

虫を探して歩いた秋の1日も、そろそろ夕闇が迫ってきました。
引き上げようかなと斜面を下っているとき、白く光るものが見えました。
近づいてみると、2頭のチョウがメヒシバの穂の先になかよくならんでとまっています。
風で揺れても飛び立つ気配がありません。多分このまま夜を過ごすのでしょう。大きさは12ミリほど。
幼虫はカタバミを食べて育つので人家の近くで普通に見られます。

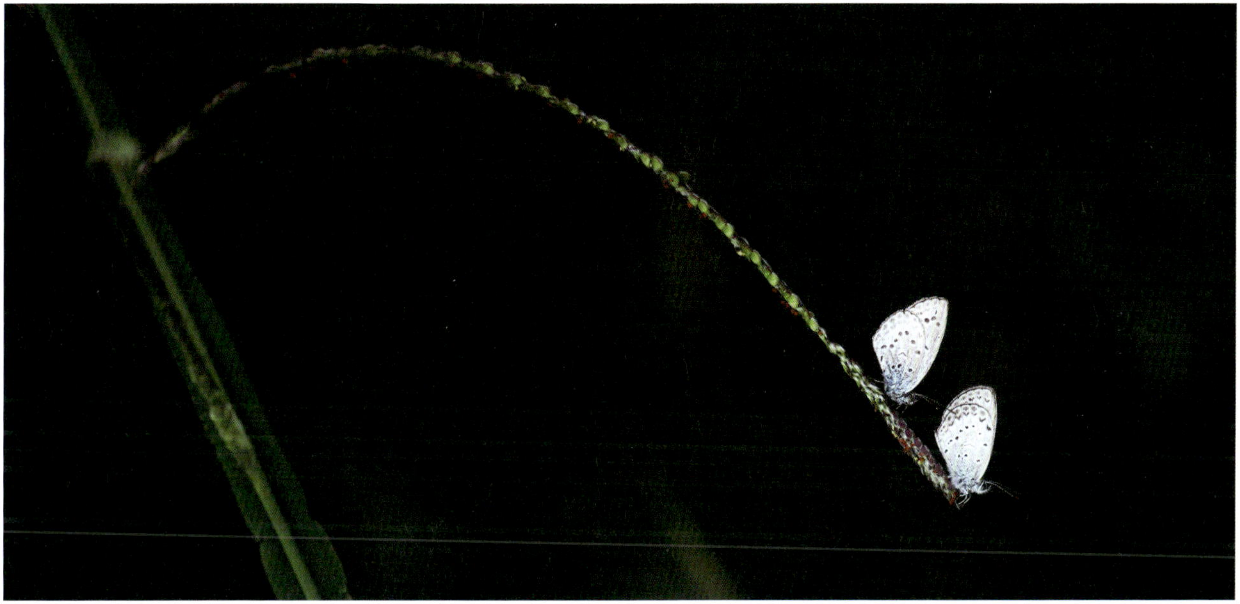

Pseudozizeeria maha / Grass blue butterfly (November, Kyushu)　ヤマトシジミ（11月 鹿児島県）

A restaurant packed under clear autumn blue sky is rated five-star

満席の　秋晴れ食堂
五つ星

The season of double-spotted swertia has come and
the both sides of the forest road along the river were covered by their star-shaped flowers.
There are five petals in the flower and its nectar is said to come out from the green spots of each petal.
Flowers are designed to let insects lick their nectar so that their body touches stamens and pistils.
But insects like small ants lick nectar without pollinating
which make them unwelcomed to flowers.

川沿いの林道はちょうどアケボノソウの季節。
路の両側に星のような花をたくさん開いています。蜜は5つの花びらのそれぞれに2つずつある
丸い緑色の部分から出ているそうで、虫たちがなめようとすると、お腹が花の中心にある
雄しべや雌しべに触れるように工夫されているのだそうです。でも小さなアリたちは、しべに
触れることなくなめるので、花にとっては蜜だけ盗られる迷惑な存在です。

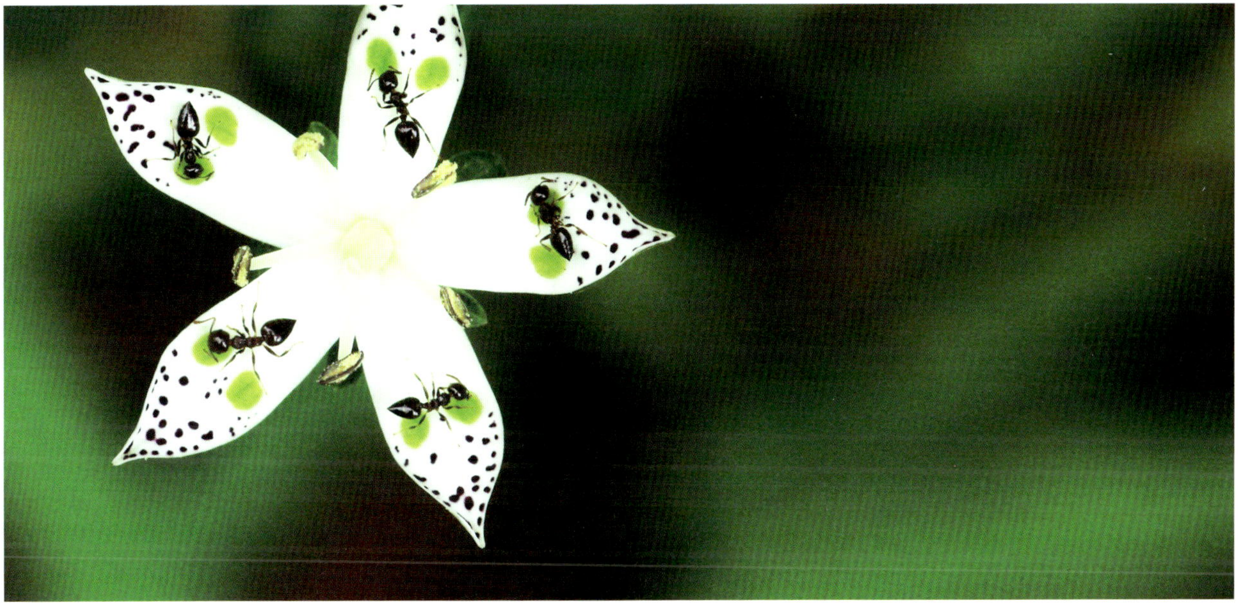

Formicidae sp. / Ant (October, Kyushu)　アリの一種（10月 鹿児島県）

Two helicopters
flying side by side
never to leave one another

双胴の　ヘリコプターだ
右ひだり

Bee flies hover around tiny flowers so quickly that they only allow us to anticipate lucky moments of coincidental focus. But the pair is slightly less nimble. We can enjoy watching them because autumn is the season of love. The pair in this photo was about to move onto another flower in front of a guard rail along forest path. The female seemed addicted to nectar while the male was trying to drag her from the flower and fly to the opposite side. Their long-stretched dangling hind legs with yellow socks look so cool.

小さな花の周りをすばしこく飛びまわるので、たまたまピントが合うのを期待するしかありませんが、ペアは少し動きが遅くなります。秋にはペアが多くなるので楽しみです。これは林道の汚れたガードレールの前で、別の花に移ろうとしているところ。蜜にこだわるのはメス。オスは花から引き離すように反対側に飛ぼうとします。だらりと伸ばした長い後ろ脚の黄色いソックスがすてきです。

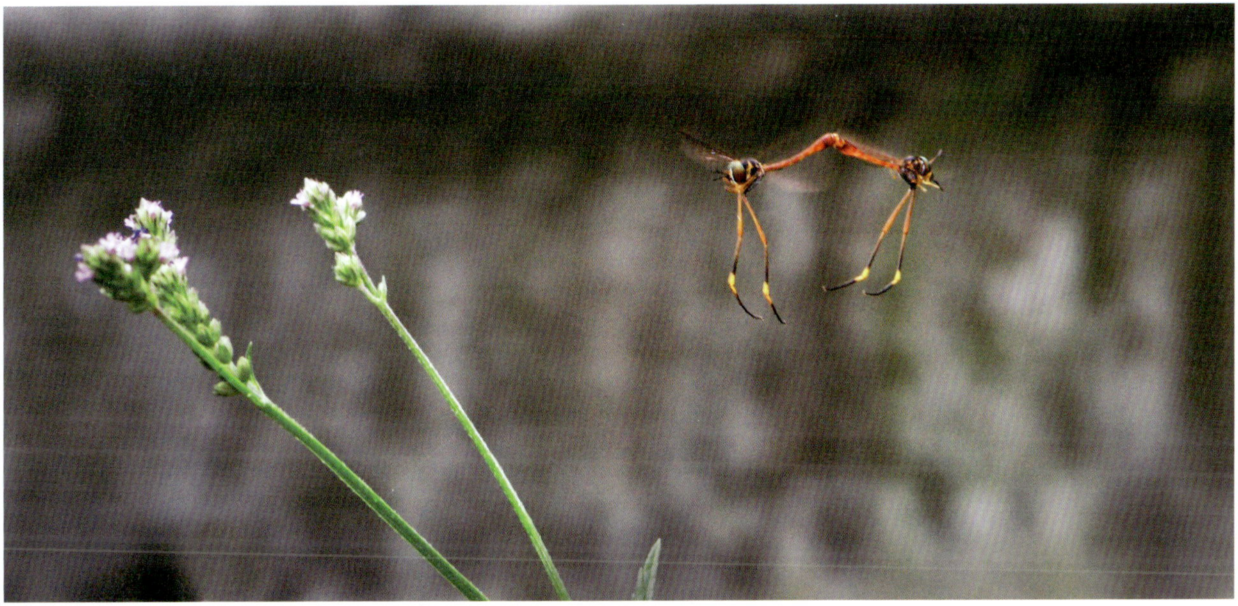

Systropus sp. / Bee fly (October, Kyushu)　ハラボソツリアブの一種（10月 鹿児島県）

In the evening dusk
a life is being passed down
upon the aqua

夕まぐれ　生命継ぎおり
水の上

I dropped by the aqua garden after watching insects all day, hoping I have come at the right time.
I went straight to the waterway and there she was. A damselfly was just about to lay eggs.
As autumn deepened, they usually lays eggs from evening to night on branches
stretching above the water. Larvae emerged from eggs can go into water when they fall from branches.
But as it was a dry bamboo, she flew away soon though she was ready to lay eggs.
The branch may have been too hard for her to attach eggs on.

1日遊んでの帰りに、水生植物園に立ち寄りました。
そろそろかなあといつもの水路に行くと、やっぱりいました。秋も深くなると産卵が始まります。
産卵はいつも夕方から夜にかけて、水の上に張り出している木の枝です。
孵化した幼虫はそのまま落ちれば水の中です。でもこれは枯れた竹。産卵体制に入りましたが、
ちょっと硬かったのでしょう、すぐに飛んで行ってしまいました。

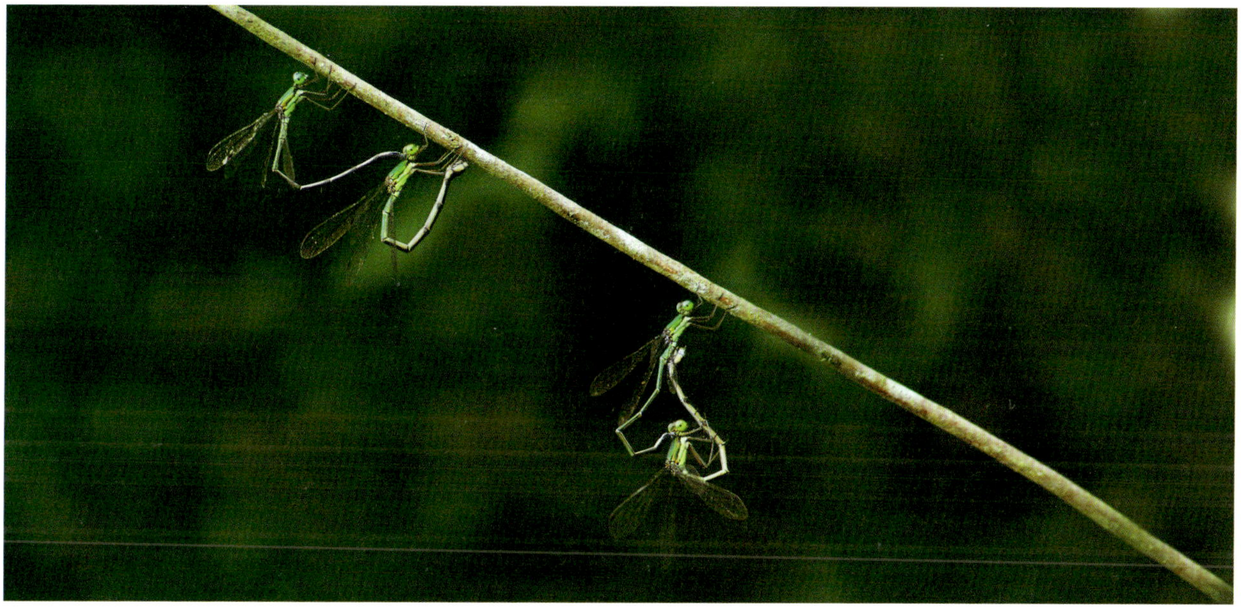

Lestes temporalis / Large emerald damselfly (October, Kyushu)　オオアオイトトンボ（10月 鹿児島県）

Still in doze
are dews in the grass
autumn clears the air

まだ覚めぬ　くさむらの露
秋気澄む

It was a chilly morning and dews fell on a vacant land next to my house covered with summer grass. I walked in and to my surprise I found a large number of derbid plant-hoppers that I had seen only once before that morning. I was really happy to find so many of them in my neighborhood. They have crossed eyes, a round-shaped body of about 4 mm in length and wings more than twice as long as their body. They generally suck sap of silver grass and are seen from summer to early autumn.

今朝は冷え込んで、夏草が茂ったままの隣の空き地に露が降りました。長靴を履いて入ってみると、思いがけず、それまで１度しか見たことがなかったアカハネナガウンカがたくさん見つかりました。こんなに身近なところで会えるなんて感激です。寄り目で丸っこい体は体長４ミリほど。その倍以上の長い翅を持っています。ススキなどの汁を吸い、夏から秋口に見られることが多いそうです。

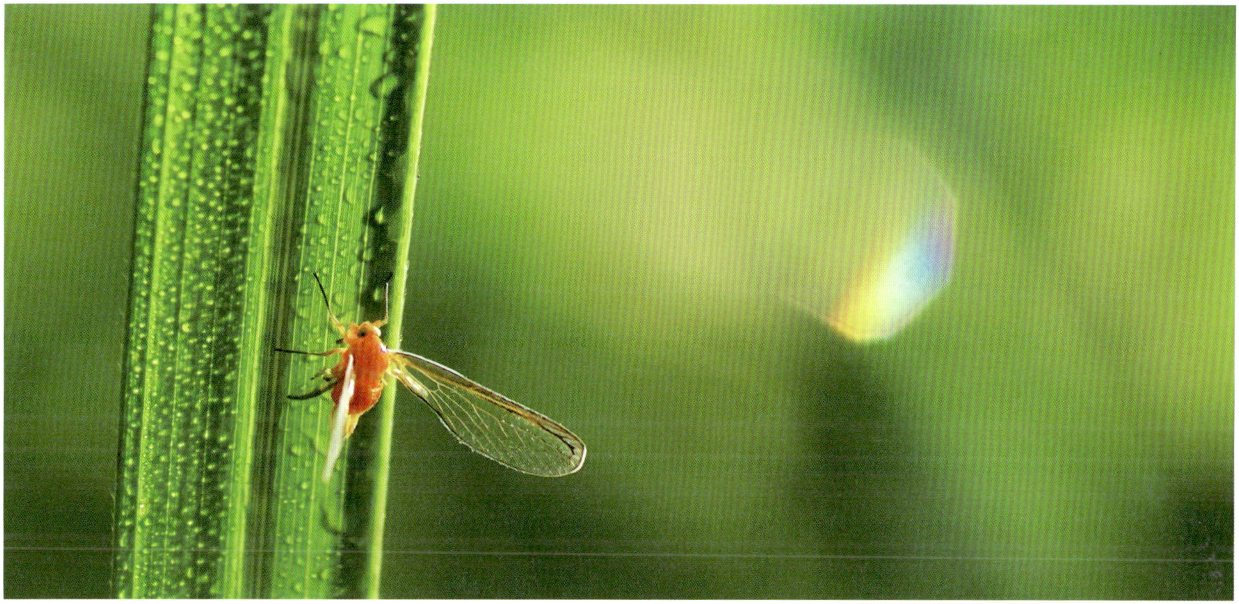

Diostrombus politus / Derbid planthopper (September, Kyushu)　アカハネナガウンカ（9月 鹿児島県）

Among silver grass
the wings glitter
autumn night falls

ススキ野に　翅かがやかせ
秋暮れる

The sun was setting and I was hurrying home.
Just then I found something glittering on a leaf of a silver grass against the sun.
Looking through the lens, I saw an incredibly large planthopper; a size I had never seen.
Obstructed by a cliff, I could not position myself very well but still I carefully focused on him and took the shot. Their body length is about 5 mm and their wings 17 mm.
Larvae are said to feed on fungi.

もう夕方になりました。足を速めて歩いていると、
逆光のススキの葉でなにか光っています。もしかするとハネナガウンカ?
レンズで覗くと、今まで見たことのない大きなハネナガウンカです。崖の近くなので思うような
ポジションをとれませんが、慎重にピントを合わせてシャッターを押します。体長は5ミリ程ですが、
翅の長さは17ミリ程もあります。幼虫はキノコ類を食べるといわれています。

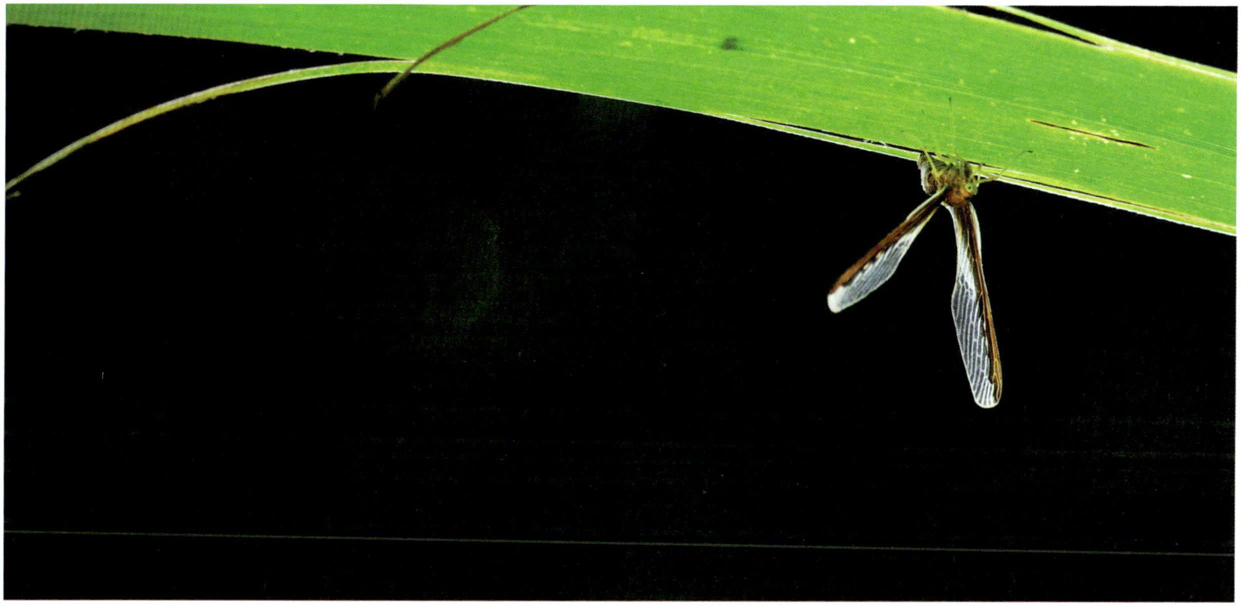

Zoraida pterophaoroides / Planthopper (October, Kyushu)　マエグロハネナガウンカ（10月 鹿児島県）

Celestial light trapped in a pond of autumn

天穹の　光つつみし
池の秋

There is a small pond in the allotment garden nearby. A meadowhawk came to sit on a dry grass.
I pressed the shutter button from the edge of the pond letting the sun's reflection in the framework.
Meadowhawk is characterized by the vivid red color of its body and beautiful orange color at the
basal of the wings. Their body length is about 40 mm, they live from the main island to Kyushu region.
They emerge in early summer, live a while in the woods and in autumn they return to
ponds or marshes with their body turned red.

市民農園の中に小さな池があります。巡回していたネキトンボが枯れ草の上にとまりました。
池の縁から、太陽の反射を入れてシャッターを押します。
アカネの中でも体の赤が鮮やかで、翅の付け根も橙色に染まっていてきれいです。
大きさ40ミリほどで、本州から九州にすんでいます。初夏に羽化するそうですが、
しばらくは林の中で生活し、秋になると体を赤く染めて池や沼に戻ってきます。

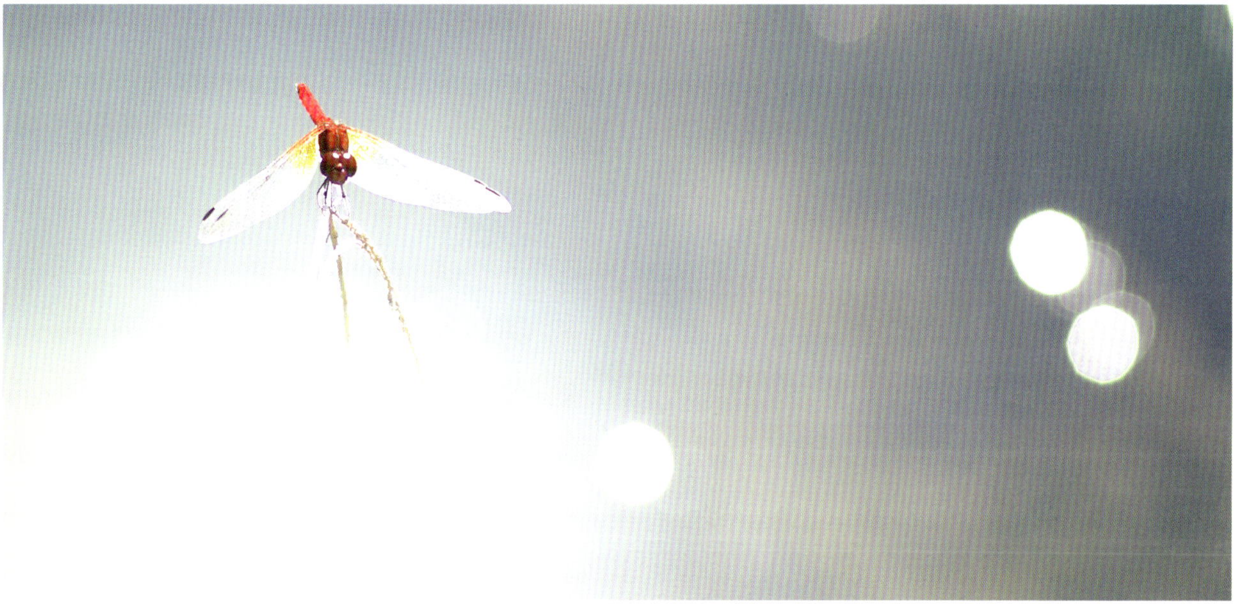

Sympetrum speciosum / Meadowhawk (October, Kyushu)　ネキトンボ（10月 鹿児島県）

Turn to starboard!
Sky is clear and weather is fair
over the little ocean

右せんかーい　視界良好
池の秋

In balmy days of autumn, darters ready to lay eggs swarmed around a little pond in the waterway.
They often lay eggs around noon. Waterweed were creating beautiful patterns and
I pressed the shutter button toward the bright surface reflecting sunshine.
Banded darters have a brownish band from stigma*5 to the center of the wing which creates
a circle when they hover. Males with their red abdomen and head are exquisite.
They live from Hokkaido to Kyushu.

今日は小春日和*6です。用水路の途中の小さな池は、産卵するアカネたちでにぎわっています。
産卵は暖かな真昼の時間帯が多いようです。反射でまぶしい水面に向けてシャッターを押したら、
水草が模様を作ってくれました。このアカネは翅の縁紋*7から内側にかけて褐色の帯があり、
ホバリングすると輪を描きます。成熟したオスは顔までまっ赤でとてもきれいです。
北海道から九州にすんでいます。

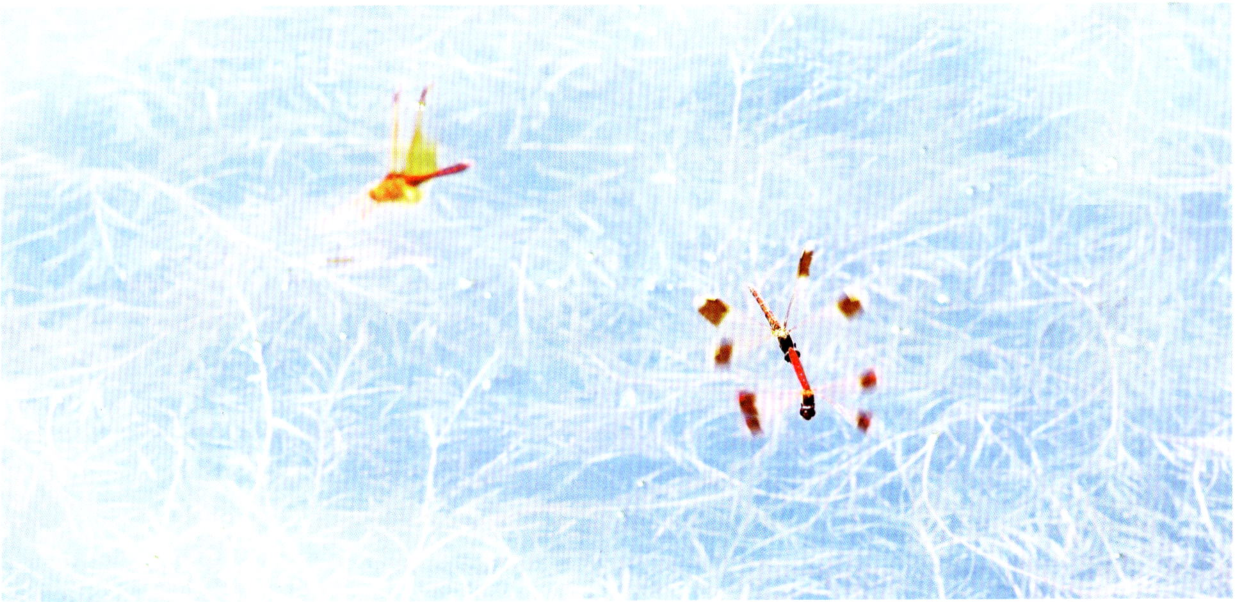

Sympetrum pedemontanum and Sympetrum croceolum / Banded darter and Yellow darter (October, Kyushu)
ミヤマアカネ(ボケているのはキトンボ)(10月 鹿児島県)

Autumn to Winter

秋から冬へ

Drizzling rain shed colored leaves.

時雨がもみじ葉を
落とします

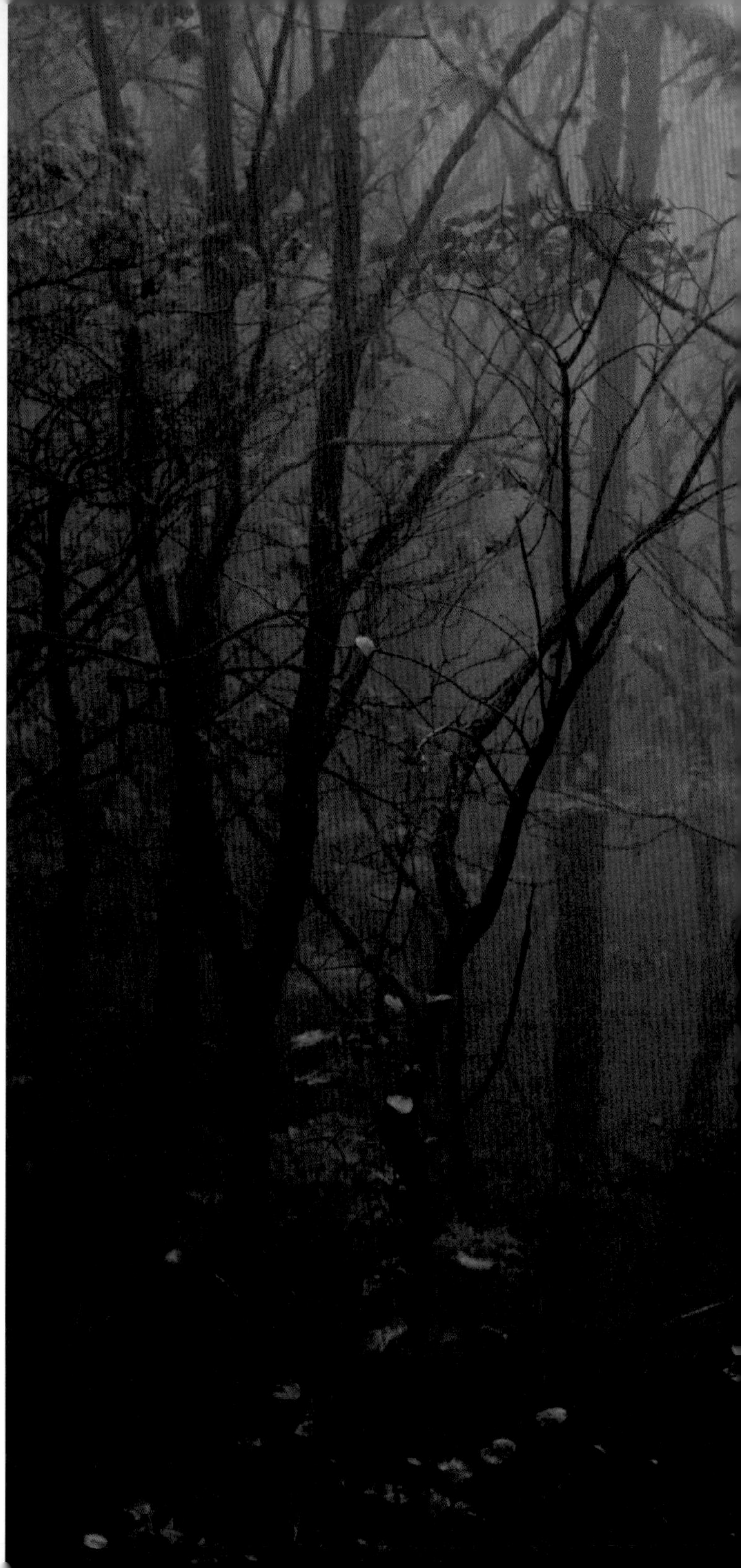

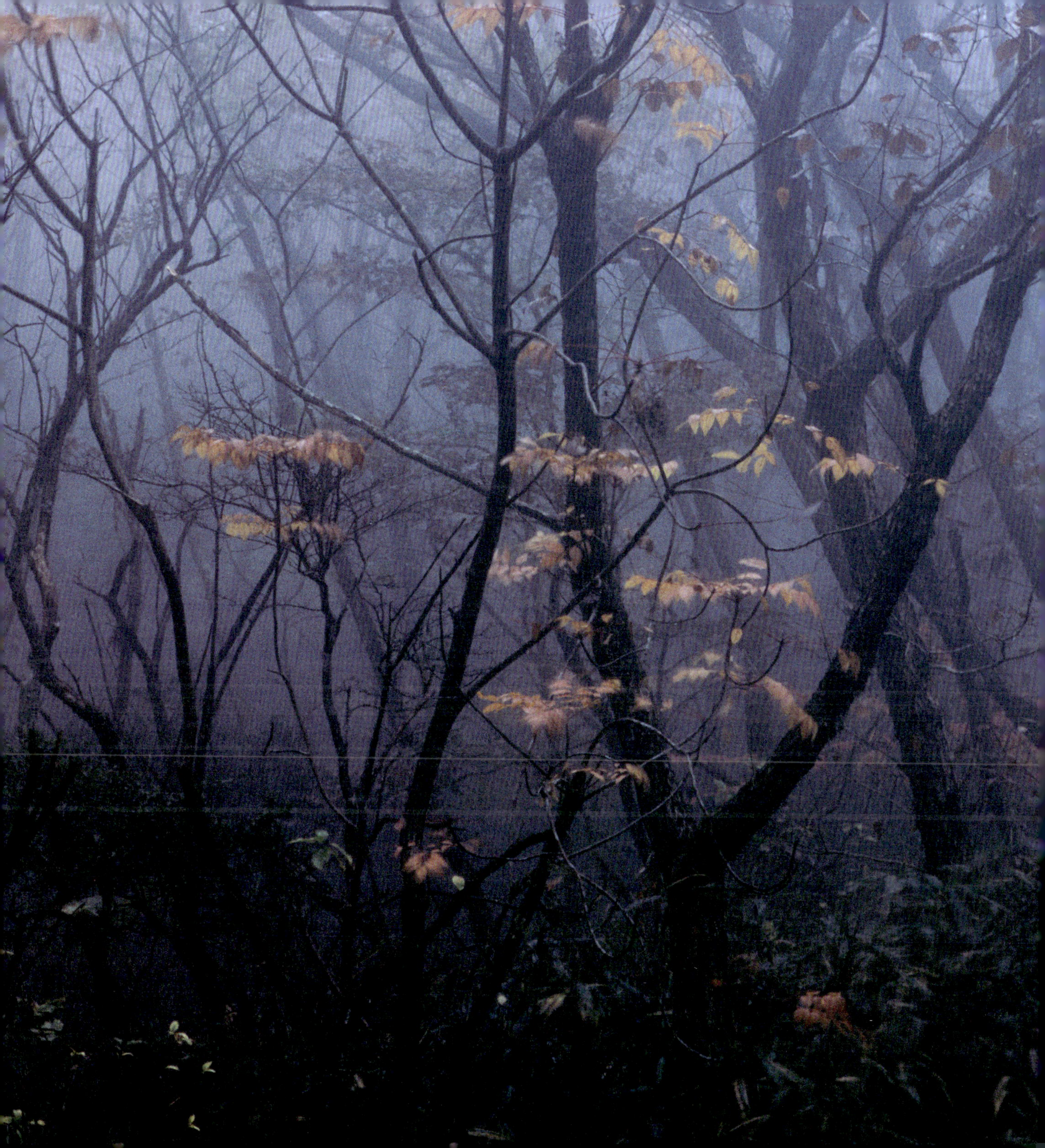

Under thousands of stars
a final task in life
is about to begin

星原や　終の務めも
遠からじ

After the frost-descent period*8 I went out to the waterways to observe dragonflies but I found a pregnant mantis instead.
As it was getting colder night by night the mantis would probably die within days.
Before she dies a final duty awaits her; making egg-case to carry on to the next generation.
In spring, hundreds of larvae will be born from one egg-case. I took a photo of the galaxy after waiting until dark and tried to make a composite photo with the mantis.

霜降*9も過ぎたころ、トンボの観察に出かけた水路でお腹の大きなカマキリを見つけました。
夜の寒さも厳しくなり、生命が終わるのもそう遠くはないでしょう。
その前に次の命を引き継ぐための卵鞘*10を作る最後の仕事をしなければなりません。
春には1つの卵鞘から数百匹の幼虫が生まれます。
暗くなるまで待って銀河を撮り、カマキリとの合成を試みました。

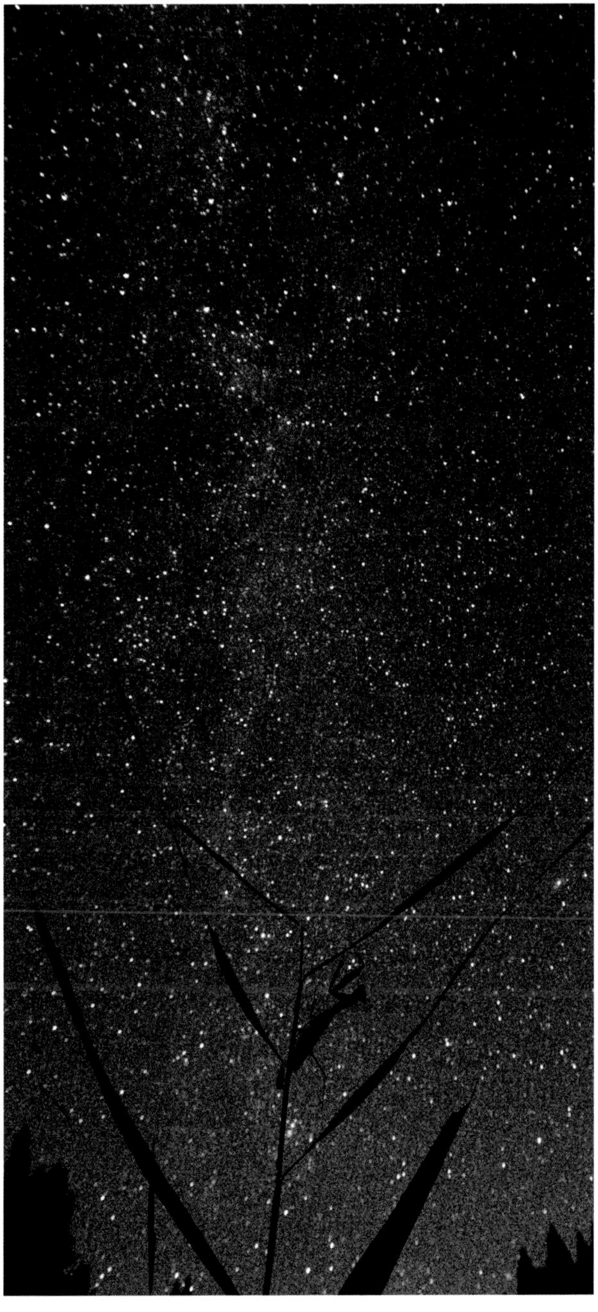

Mantodea sp. / Mantis
(October, Kyushu)
カマキリの一種（10月 鹿児島県）

Pieces from the sun are shining so bright on Okinawan hibiscus

太陽の　かけらを乗せる 島芙蓉

Okinawan hibiscus were in full bloom in the park with its
pale pink flowers offering insects spots as restaurant or for match-making.
Particularly, red cotton stainers outnumbered among them. Whenever I see them,
their tropical outfit with a black pattern on their red body reminds me that I am on a tropical island.
They say they don't smell awful like any other stink bugs although I have never tried taking them in my hand.
Their body length is about 15 mm and they live on Ryukyu Islands.

公園には、薄桃色のサキシマフヨウの花がたくさん咲いていて、
虫たちの食堂や出会いの場になっています。特に多いのがこのカメムシ。
まっ赤な体に黒い模様のあるいかにも南国の虫らしいいでたちで、
会うたびに南の島に来たんだなあという実感がわきます。私は手にとって嗅いだことはありませんが、
カメムシ特有の臭い匂いはしないそうです。大きさ15ミリほど。琉球列島にすんでいます。

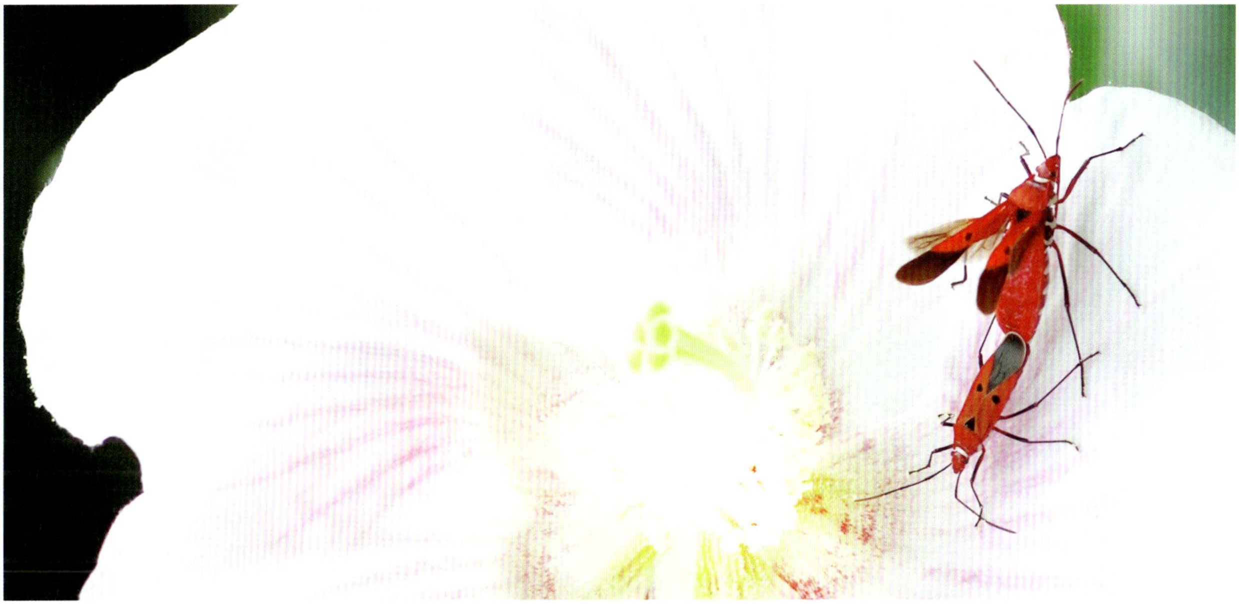

Dysdercus cingulatus / Red cotton stainer (November, Ishigaki Island / Okinawa)　アカホシカメムシ（11月中旬 石垣島）

Even dressed in gold
hiding from the world
can be the answer

金襴の　身も隠れたい
時がある

On the backside of a leaf, I happened to find a bug of golden green.
I am fully aware the photo here would not express the glitter of the insect.
But you would not have that glitter either even in a specimen because colors change.
Therefore, it is really worth visiting Yaeyama and seeing them alive.
Jewel bugs are not rare and they are seen to form a group of several tens of them.
Their body length is about 18 mm and they are seen in Nansei Islands throughout the year.

公園の出口付近の葉の裏で、金緑色に輝くカメムシを見つけました。
でも、写真ではその輝きは十分には伝わりません。標本も色が変わってしまいます。
八重山に行ってぜひ本物の生きている姿を見てみてください。
珍しいものではなく、時に数10匹もの集団を作ることもあるそうです。
大きさ18ミリほど。南西諸島にすんでいて、年中見ることができます。

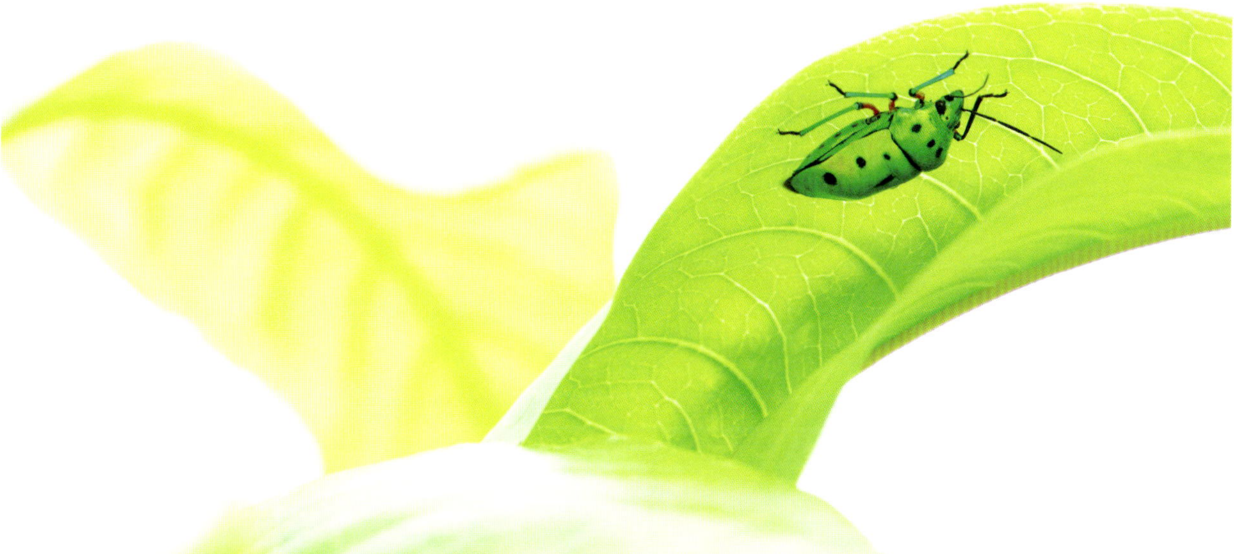

Calliphara exellens / Jewel bug (November, Ishigaki Island / Okinaka)　ナナホシキンカメムシ（11月中旬 石垣島）

Two mates wearing the same clothes white gloves and tabis

あいぼうも　白い手袋
白い足袋

I was bothered by muzzling sky and strong wind during my last trip to Yaeyama.
Slender flies came to console me walking on a forest path under a drizzle.
They always twitch their front legs in white gloves in front of
their face like antennae as if they mimic bees.
Large leaves of Alocasia here and there were offering stage for them to perform.
They live in Ryukyu Islands.

今回の八重山の旅は、小雨模様の空と強い風に悩まされました。
霧雨の林道を歩いていると、あちこちでこのヤセバエが出てきて慰めてくれました。
白い手袋をした前脚をいつも顔の前で触角のようにぴろぴろさせているのは、
ハチをまねているのでしょうか。ところどころにクワズイモが大きな葉を広げていて、
舞台を提供してくれています。琉球列島にすんでいます。

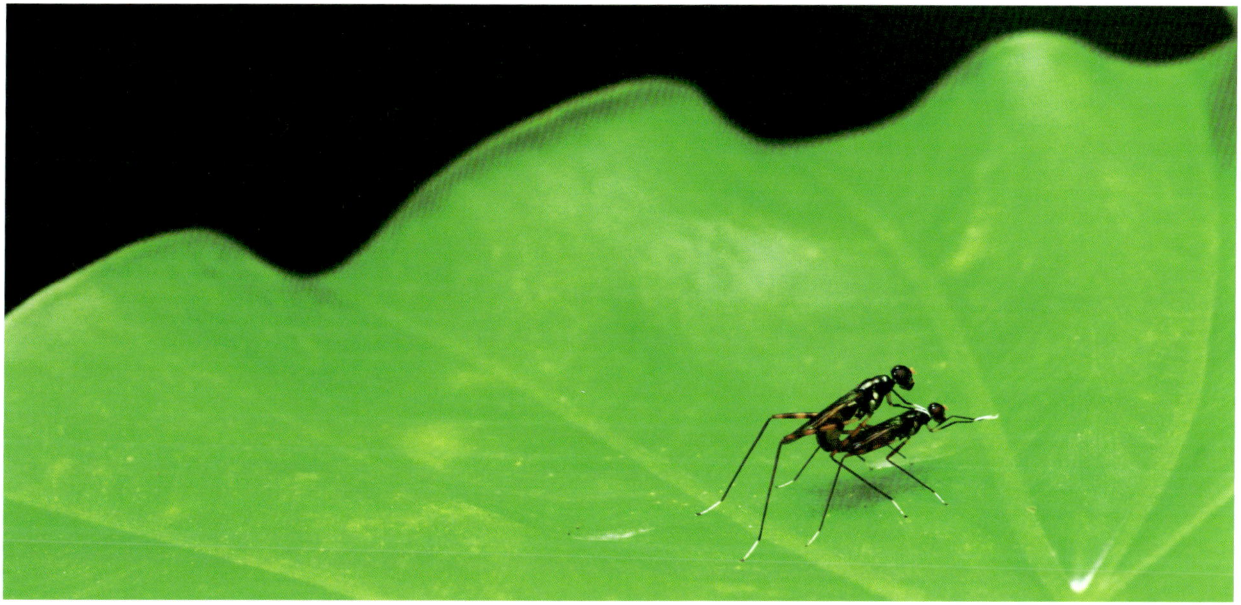

Gymnonerius sp. / Slender fly (November, Iriomote Island / Okinawa)　マダラアシナガヤセバエ(11月中旬 西表島)

Imminent danger
may happen at any time
you can't be too careful

一寸の　先は危険が
あぶないよ

I found mantidflies on leaves of alocasia and other flowers during my visit to Ishigaki Island and Iriomote Island. Mantidflies look like mantis at a first glance but they are actually close to mayflies. If you look closely you will see that their abdomen and wings resemble those of mayflies, whereas their way of catching insects with their sickle-like forelegs is the same as that of mantis. Larvae grow in their unique way of sucking fluids of spiders and liquids of spiders' eggs. There are six of its kind in Japan.

石垣島と西表島に行ったとき、花の近くやクワズイモの葉の上でカマキリモドキに会うことができました。一見カマキリのように見えますが、アミメカゲロウに近いそうです。そういえば体や翅はカゲロウですね。でも鎌で虫を捕える方法はカマキリと同じです。幼虫の生活が変わっていて、ほとんどはクモの体液や卵の汁を吸って成長するそうです。日本には、同じ仲間が6種ほどいるそうです。

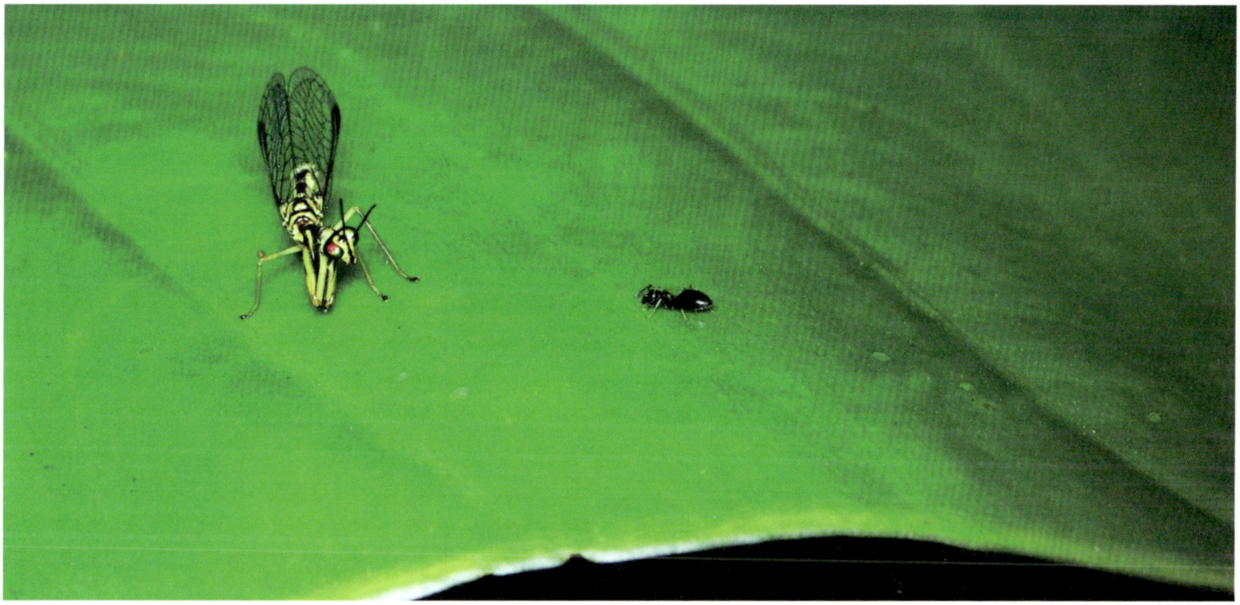

Mantispa transversa / Mantidfly (November, Iriomote Island / Okinawa)　ミナミヒメカマキリモドキ（11月下旬 西表島）

Putting this world behind alone in the heaven of southern island

うつし世を　離れて冬の南ぬ島

I visited Yaeyama Island around the coldest season of the year.
The temperature there was slightly lower than 20 °C. In winter it gets cloudy or drizzles most of the time but on fine days various insects start to fly out from here and there.
It looks like heaven. I saw metalmark moths shining on beautiful white flowers of beggarticks.
They are commonly seen and they always welcome me whenever I go. Their body length is about 10 mm.
They feed on ficus and are seen throughout the year.

大寒のころ、八重山に行きました。気温は20度弱。
島の冬は小雨や曇り空が多いのですが、たまに晴れると、あちこちから飛びだす虫たちで天国のようになります。センダングサの白い花で、きらきら光るハマキモドキを見つけました。
珍しいものではなく、ミドリオオハマキモドキとともにいつも歓迎してくれます。
大きさ10ミリほど。オオバイヌビワを食べ、年中見ることができます。

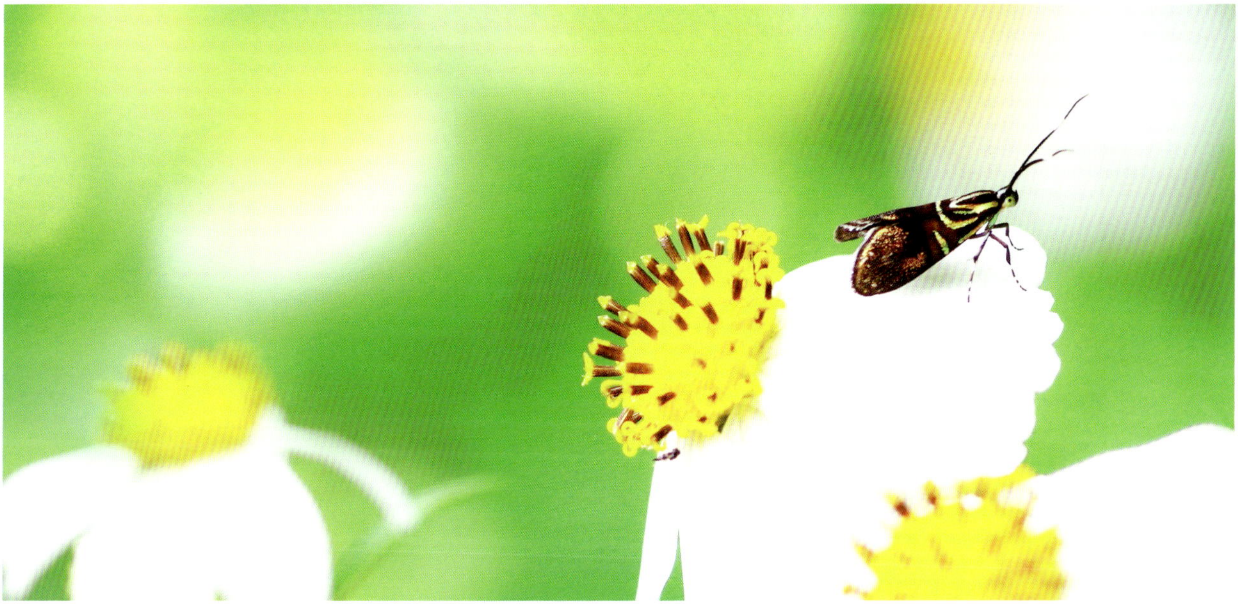

Saptha divitiosa / Metalmark moth (February, Ishigaki Island / Okinawa)　イヌビワオオハマキモドキ（2月初旬 石垣島）

In forests of Amami
butterflies slumber
winter treats them gently

蝶ねむる　奄美の森の
冬やさし

Seeking butterflies of the cold season, I traveled with a photo-lover friend of mine to Amami Island. Guided by a local photographer we came to a forest where we were surrounded by hundreds of butterflies hanging on branches. In the morning most of them were closing their wings but as the temperature rose they floated in the air around us. It was as if we were in a fairy land. Ceylon blue glassy tiger is seen active in Nansei Islands all year round.

寒い時期だけに見られるチョウの集団に会いたくて、写友と２人で奄美大島へ出かけました。地元の写真家に案内してもらった森には、本当に何百というチョウがあちこちの木枝にぶら下がっています。朝方は翅を閉じていますが、昼ごろになって気温が上がると、たくさんのチョウがふわふわと私たちのまわりを飛び回り、まるでおとぎの国にいるようでした。南西諸島では、年中活動しています。

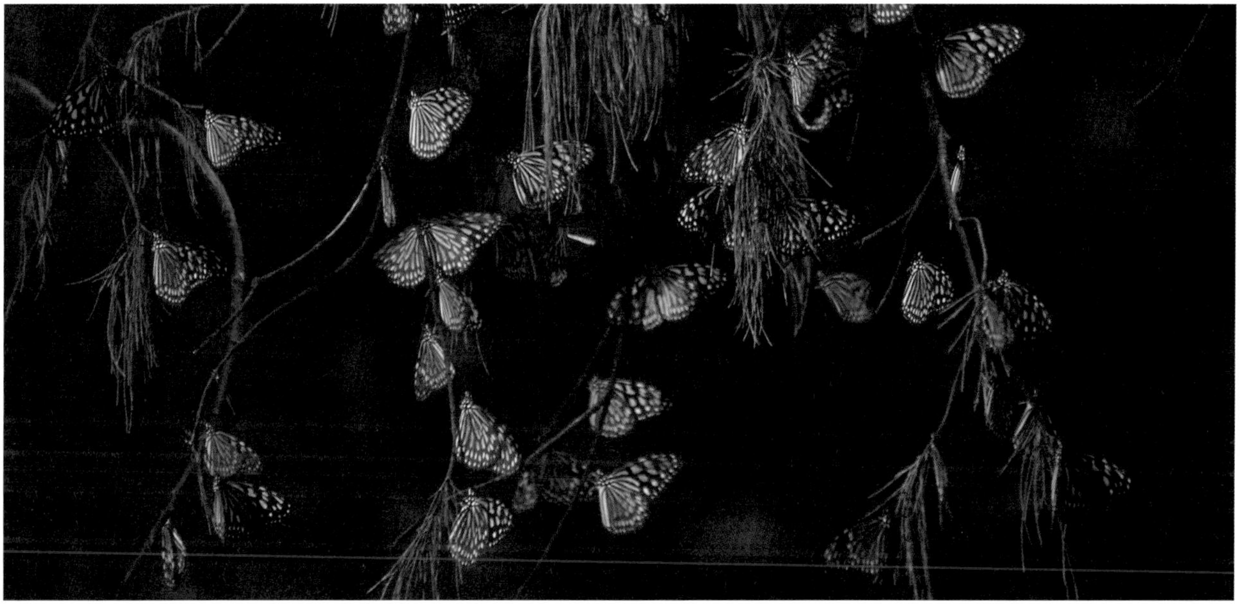

Ideopsis similis / Ceylon blue glassy tiger (February, Amami Oshima Island / Kyushu)　リュウキュウアサギマダラ（2月 奄美大島）

Winter to Spring

冬から春へ

The soft fog covers mountain villages.

ふんわりとした霧が
山里を覆います

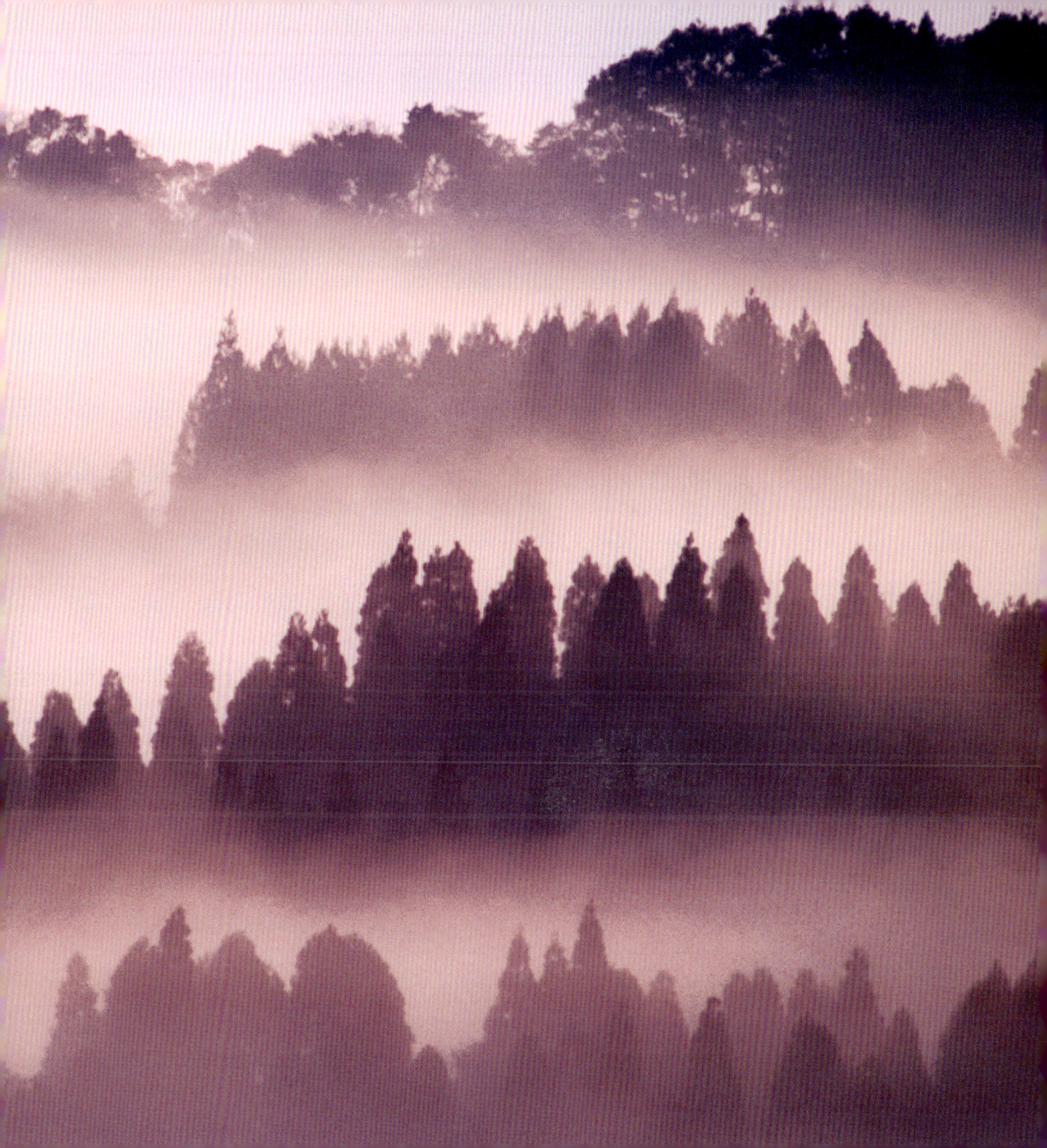

Life since ancient times
is inherited here in a stream of spring
with the chilly air from the mountains

いにしえの　生命継ぎおり　山深き
つめたき風の　春の小川に

On a wood trunk by the stream, I found a deep-black larva of dragonfly.
It took about 15 minutes to have his body crawl out of his old skin after his back had split.
Then resting for nearly an hour, he pulled out his tail and stretched his wings while clinging to
his cast-off skin. It was obvious it would take the entire day for him to fly out in the sky.
The fossils of the ancient dragonfly were discovered in strata of Triassic and Jurassic periods. They have shape
similar to clubtail dragonfly and wings similar to those of emerald damselfly. They are endemic to Japan.

渓流沿いの木の幹で、まっ黒なヤゴを見つけました。
背中が割れ始めてから上半身を出すのに15分ほど。仰向けで1時間近く休んでから尾を抜き、
羽化殻につかまって翅をのばします。飛び立つのは明日になるかもしれません。
三畳紀とジュラ紀の地層から化石が見つかっていて、体形はサナエトンボに、
翅形はアオイトトンボに似ている不思議なトンボです。日本だけにすんでいます。

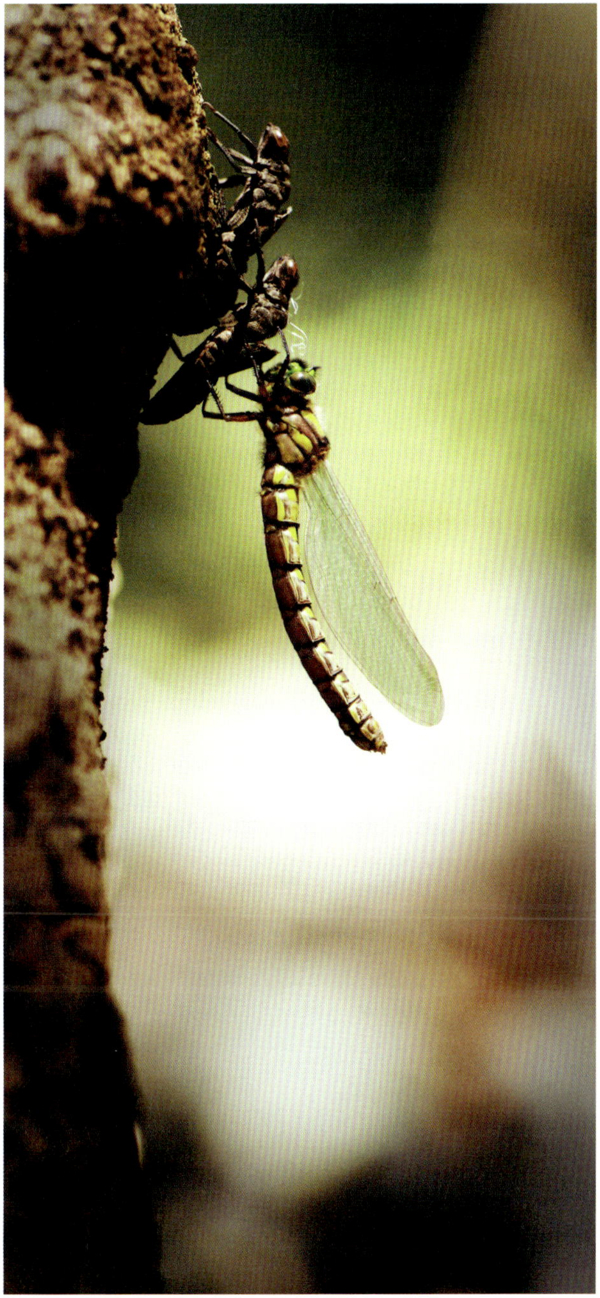

Epiophlebia superstes /
Ancient dragonfly
(March, Kyushu)
ムカシトンボ（3月中旬 鹿児島県）

Tiny little bee
dressed in smooth velvet
heralds the advent of spring

ビロードの　プチぬいぐるみ
春告げる

A long winter has finally ended. On the grassland warmed by spring sunshine, early sinicus started to pop out and insects began to show up looking buoyant and cheerful. A bee fly was stretching his long straw seeking for nectar of white cardamine. They are ephemeral*[11] and herald the coming of spring every year. Their body is covered by thin long yellow hair which looks like a stuffed animal when they are flying. They grow inside the nest of ground-nesting bees.

長い冬も終わりました。光いっぱいの野原に虫たちが姿を見せ始めて、心うきうき。気の早いレンゲソウもちらほら。白い小さなタネツケバナに、ツリアブが長いストローをのばして蜜を求めています。毎年、春を告げてくれるスプリング・エフェメラル*[12]です。細長い黄色い毛におおわれていて、ぬいぐるみが飛んでいるようです。ツリアブの仲間は、ヒメハナバチの巣などに寄生して育つそうです。

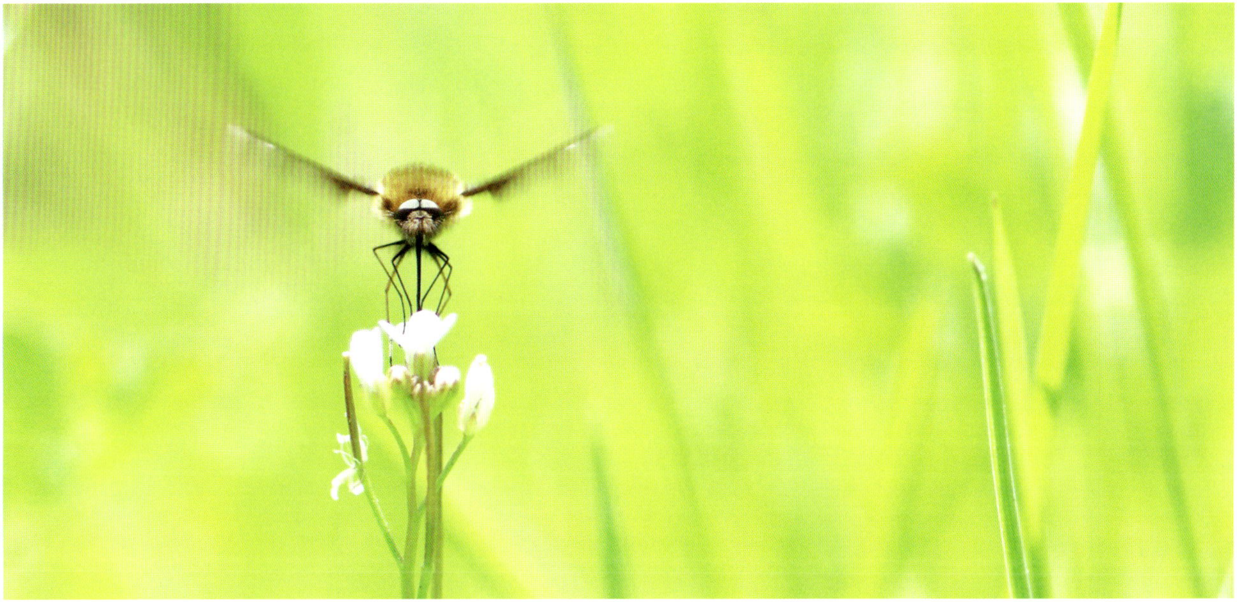

Bombylius major / Bee fly (February, Kyushu)　ビロードツリアブ（2月 鹿児島県）

Climbing up the Japan Alps to meet butterflies

There are butterflies that I yearn for and cannot meet easily due to their limited habitat and period of appearance. Mr. Mitsuru Kameyama, an expert of rare species of butterflies, took me to the dream place. He is my mentor in the field of insects and has helped me during my pursuit of gifu butterfly and trip to Indonesia (pp. 42-43). **photo A:** There is a boulder-strewn swamp about an-hour-walk from Kamonji-goya. Orange-tip butterflies, fluttering up and down the swamp, hardly stopped flying. They are often dubbed as *'Kumotsuki'* in Japan. **photo B:** Snow still remained in the valley, where I found a female orange-tip butterfly among tower-mustard growing in dense. Closing its wings with its unique inner exquisite pattern while hiding forewings under hindwings, the butterfly showed us only the green-veined pattern on the outer surface of its white-background wings. She seemed to have already gone to a dreamland. **photo C:** Around the mountain-top ran a passage of wind. By laying down its body to the ground with its wings closed, the butterfly was trying to look like a pebble. But he gave me one big chance; he opened slightly his wings for me. This butterfly, listed as one of the endangered species by the Ministry of Environment, is dubbed as *'Haimatsu sennin'* or 'a hermit living in a bush of creeping pine'.

A tiny dancer
in a swamp of melted snow
enjoys tea break

雪解けの　沢のダンサー
ティータイム

Near the mountain after dark
white field of flowers lies
far beyond horizon

山暮れて　白き花野の
夢はるか

A

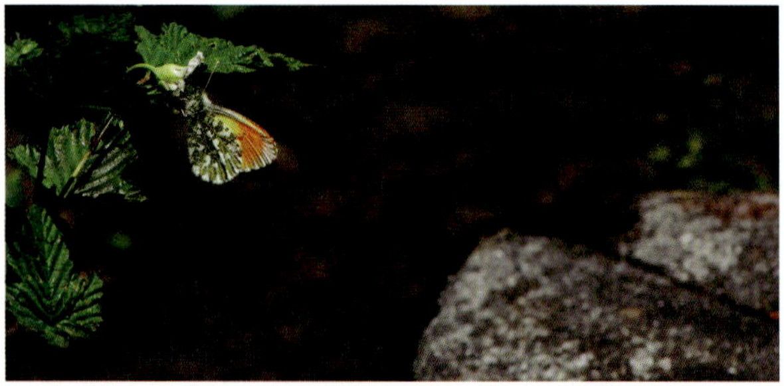

Male Anthocharis cardamines / Male Orange tip (May, Nagano)
クモマツマキチョウ雄(5月 長野県)

B

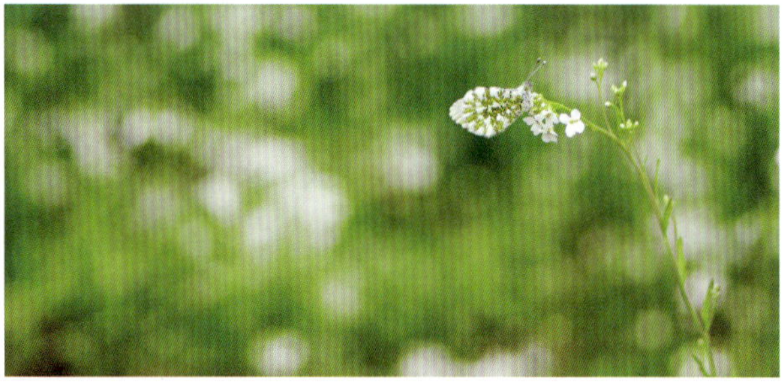

Female Anthocharis cardamines / Female Orange tip (May, Nagano)
クモマツマキチョウ雌(5月 長野県)

photo D: I chanced upon a golden butterfly of the family of gossamer-winged butterfly at a sunny scree. He appeared to be sucking water seeping through rocks. This species is also endemic to Japan.

日本アルプスの蝶に会いに

すむ場所や出現の時期が限られていて簡単には会えない憧れの蝶たちがいます。そんな蝶たちを知りつくした亀山充氏が、日本アルプスまで連れて行ってくれました。ギフチョウやインドネシア（42、43頁）でもお世話になった頼りになる虫の先輩です。**写真A：**嘉門次小屋から1時間ほど歩くと、ごろごろした岩の大きな沢に出ます。オレンジ色が沢を上ったり下ったりしていますが、なかなかとまってくれません。クモツキの愛称があります。**写真B：**谷にはまだ雪が残っています。たくさんのハタザオの中にメスを見つけました。前翅を後翅にかくして草ずり模様しか見えません。もうすっかり夢の世界に入っているようです。**写真C：**広い頂上付近は風の通り道。いつも体を地面に倒し翅を閉じて、小石と同化しています。でもちょっとだけ翅を広げてくれました。環境省指定絶滅危惧種で、ハイマツ仙人と呼ばれます。**写真D：**太陽が照りつける沢のガレ場で金色のシジミチョウを見つけました。浸み出した水を吸っているようです。日本特産種。

Wind falls silent
hermit of mountain appears
behind rocks

風やんで　仙人ひとり
岩のかげ

God of Mountain
bestows on us with his grace
a crystal-clear water

山の神　清きいずみを
与えけり

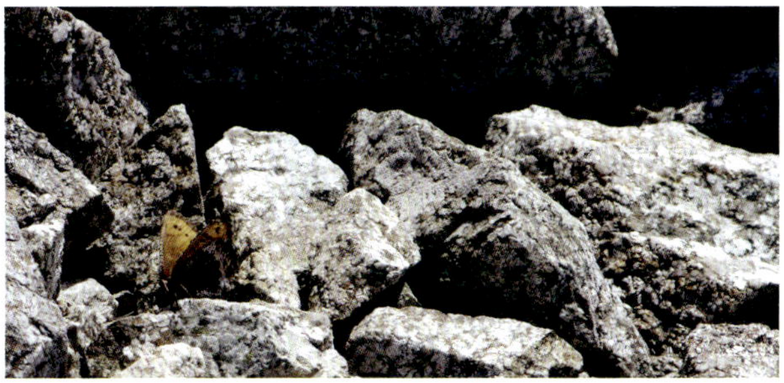

C

Oeneis norna / Norse grayling (July, Gifu)
タカネヒカゲ（7月 岐阜県）

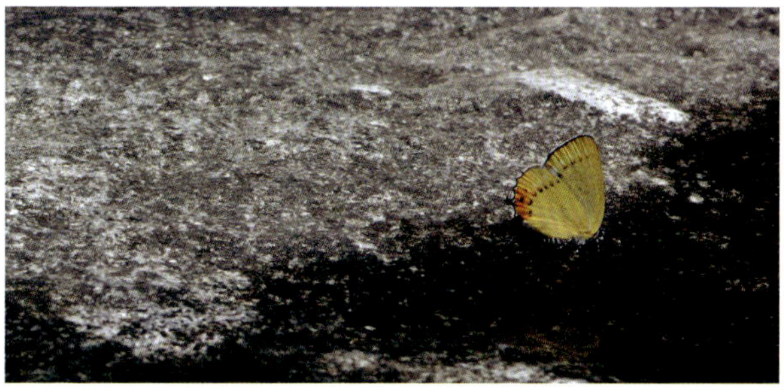

D

Ussuriana stygiana / Gossamer-winged butterfly (July, Gifu)
ウラキンシジミ（7月 岐阜県）

Looking for insects in Costa Rica

I had an opportunity to be guided by exploratory entomologist Kenji Nishida, living in Costa Rica. During the trip, I stayed at lodgings available only to researchers and spent intensive time observing insects; by walking along the insect-observation course in the daytime and with white cloths stretched almost every night. I saw many beautiful and strange insects including some 50 species of treehoppers (pp. 40-41). I was also given a warm welcome by a large number of hummingbirds. The trip to Costa Rica has become a lifelong memory for me. **photo A:** The surroundings of the Biologica Monteverde treasure so many different kind of insects and I found various species of the family of treehoppers. They have horns lighter than they look and were flitting about nimbly. **photo B:** I saw a butterfly sucking bird's dropping in the woods. Its transparent wings tend to disappear in jungles, but it stayed there for some time maybe because the droppings tasted good, allowing me to take many photos. **photo C:** At night I wandered through the woods with a flashlight looking for insects. A pair of lantern-flies were sucking sap from trees. I may have disturbed their meals. **photo D:** A leafhopper opened her wings for us just like a dancer with

Black Eboshi hat
would not bother him from walking around
though heavy it may seem

重そうな　黒い烏帽子も
気にしない

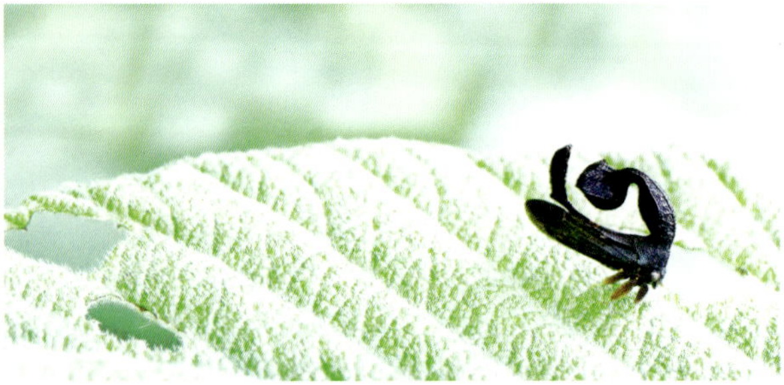

A

Cladonota sp. / Planthopper (July, Monteverde / Costa Rica)
ミカヅキツノゼミの一種(7月 モンテベルデ／コスタリカ)

Lunch in jungles
a Ninja is ready to have anything
even the most sour foods

ジャングルの　忍者の食事
すっぱそう

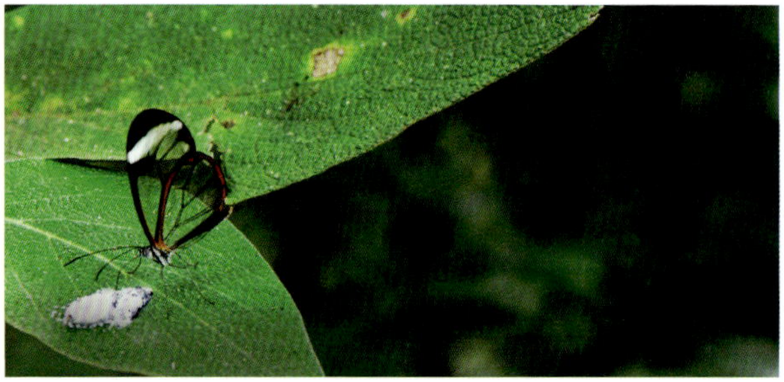

B

Greta oto / Glasswinged butterfly (July, Monteverde / Costa Rica)
ツマジロスカシマダラ(7月 モンテベルデ／コスタリカ)

crimson dress. I found her on a leaf of a tree in the garden of the Organization for Tropical Studies (OTS) in Sarapiqui.

コスタリカの虫たち

コスタリカ在住の探検昆虫学者西田賢司氏に、現地の虫たちを案内していただきました。研究者しか利用できない宿舎に泊まって観察ルートを歩き、夜もほとんど毎日白布を張って虫を観察しました(40、41頁)。50種ほどものツノゼミをはじめ、きれいでへんな虫たちばかり。たくさんのハチドリも歓迎してくれて、一生の思い出になりました。**写真A:**モンテベルデ熱帯生物研究施設のまわりは虫の宝庫。ツノゼミもいろんな種類が見つかりました。角は見かけによらず軽いようで、すばしこく飛び回ります。**写真B:**森の中で、鳥のフンを吸っているところを見つけました。透明の翅はジャングルの中ではすぐ消えてしまいますが、よほどおいしいのでしょう、何枚もシャッターを押すことができました。**写真C:**懐中電灯を持って森の中を歩いて夜の虫たちを探します。2頭でなかよく木の汁を吸っていましたが、ちょっと食事の邪魔をしたみたいです。**写真D:**サラピキ熱帯生物研究所の庭の木の葉で、真っ赤な服を着た踊り子が、翅を広げてくれました。

Sisters side by side
in the dark of the forest
where goblins dwell

魔物棲む　森の暗やみ
あねいもと

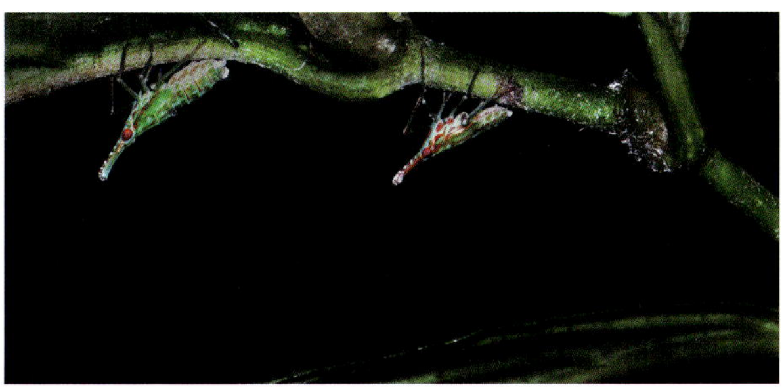

C

Fulgoridae sp. / Lanternfly (July, Monteverde / Costa Rica)
ビワハゴロモの一種の幼虫(7月 モンテベルデ／コスタリカ)

A dress of crimson
tailor made by the house of flower
of endless summer

常夏の　花からもらった
赤いべべ

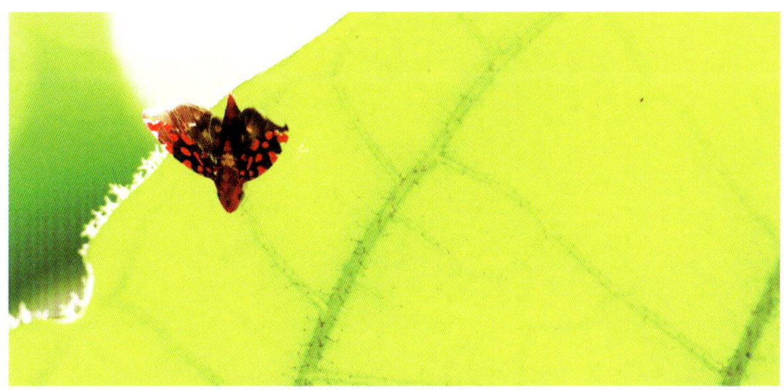

D

Cicadellidae sp. / Leafhopper (July, Sarapiqui OTS / Costa Rica)
ヨコバイの一種(7月 サラピキ熱帯生物研究所／コスタリカ)

References (*by order of appearance*)

注釈文

P 6 空天(くうてん)は、ひろびろとした空、大空。

P 8 *1 ソフトレンズは、輪郭の周りを少しぼかして柔らかな感じにするレンズです。

P 10 Hina dolls are Emperor and Empress dolls that Japanese decorate to celebrate the Doll Festival on March 3rd.

P 12 *2 ノートルダムのせむし男は、ヴィクトル・ユーゴーの小説の名前です。

P 16 清和月(せいわづき)は、陰暦4月のこと。

P 18 清風(せいふう)は、清らかな風。さわやかな風。
天馬(てんま)は、伝説上の翼のある馬。非常に優れた馬の意味もあります。
遼空(りょうくう)は、はるかにひろがる空。遠い空。

P 20 九天(きゅうてん)は、高い空・天上。

P 26 Hakkeyoi is a phrase shouted by a sumo referee during a bout, particularly when the bout has reached a standstill, to urge the wrestlers to liven up the fight. It means: "Put some spirit into it!"

P 28 Yukata is traditional Japanese cotton kimono worn by men and women in summer.

P 30 白雨は、明るい空から降る雨、にわか雨。

P 32 自立自尊は、人に頼らず自分で事を行い、自己の人格・尊厳を保つこと。福沢諭吉が創始者である慶応義塾の教育の基本になっています。

P 36 *3 同定は、生物の属や種名を決定すること。

P 44 There is a float decorated with flowers in Japan carrying offerings of food and drink to Gods. Flower floats parade with ox carts and children dressed in kimonos in a historical festival of Kyoto.
花車(はなぐるま)は、京都のお祭りで神饌(しんせん:神に供える飲食物)を運ぶ車のことで、牛車や稚児などとともに行列を作ります。

P 46 美ら島(ちゅらしま)の、「美ら」は南の島の方言で、「美しい」という意味です。
*4 縹色(はなだいろ)は、明度の高い薄青色。露草色。

P48 日盛りは、太陽が照りつける夏の午後の暑い盛り。

P56 Tengu refers to a long-nosed bird-like legendary goblin which often appears in Japanese folk beliefs and tales.
翡翠(ひすい)は、緑色の透明感のある宝石。古くは玉(ぎょく)と呼ばれて珍重されました。

P58 Kannazuki is the tenth month of the Japanese old calendar. Like Minazuki, meaning June, the middle Chinese character "無" is said to be used as a phonetic symbol to mean 'of'. Accordingly, the term means 'month of gods'.
神無月は陰暦の10月のことで、"無"は水無月の無と同じく"の"を意味するという説が有力だそうです。

P70 天穹(てんきゅう)は、大空、天空。

P72 *5 Stigma is referred to as a small square mark on the slightly inner side of dragonfly's wingtip, which is said to control irregular vibration during its flight.
*6 小春日和は、晩秋から初冬にかけて現れる穏やかな暖かい晴天。小春は旧暦の10月。
*7 縁紋は、トンボの翅の先端の少し内側に付いている小さな四角い紋。飛行中の不規則な振動を調整するといわれています。

P76 *8 The frost-descent is one of the 24 solar terms used to denote the changing of the seasons. Frost-descent is around 23 or 24 of October, the period when dew changes to frost by the cold air.
*9 霜降は、24節季のひとつで、露が冷気によって霜となって降り始めるころ。10月23・24日ころにあたります。
*10 卵鞘(らんしょう)は、卵と同時に分泌される粘液が泡だって形成されます。

P82 Tabi is traditional Japanese white socks with a separation between a big toe and others, worn by men and women with traditional Japanese clothing including kimono.

P86 うつし世(現世)は、現在暮らしている世界。この世。
南ぬ島(ぱいぬじま)は、南の島。沖縄では"ぬ"は"の"を意味します。

P94 *11 Spring ephemeral is any of various woodland wildflowers and insects that appear in the early spring. They live only for a short period of time.
*12 スプリング・エフェメラル(Spring ephemeral)は、直訳すると春のはかない命。春にだけに現れる植物や虫たちをさします。

P98 Eboshi is a kind of hat worn by aristocrats and warriors from the late 8th to the early 20th century in Japan and also worn by gyoji, referees in sumo matches.

Acknowledgement

あとがきと謝辞

Walking in field, mountains and forests, I enjoy taking photos of insects while playing with them. Once my main interest was butterflies and then moved on to dragonflies. I am now enamored with tiny insects of about-10-mm size. There are innumerous kinds of insects with different lifestyles, which offer me new findings every time I take a walk in nature. I always feel grateful for insects who pose in front of the camera and I try to shoot their photos as beautifully as possible. We used to call our archipelago Akitsushima or Dragonfly Island. Japan is blessed to have four distinctly different seasons and we have insects that appear in each of the first three seasons. And for those who miss watching insects in winter time, I definitely recommend to visit Nansei Island. It is often said that photos reflect the personality of the photographer. I hope to enhance myself as much as possible by taking photos. I would appreciate any corrections from readers should my explanation about the insects were inappropriate or insufficient. Last but not least, I would like to express my sincere gratitude to ONBEAT Corporation who kindly helped me publish this landmark photobook, especially to Tomoko YAMAMOTO and Yaeko Barre KOCHI for translation into English.

野山や林道を歩いて虫たちと遊びながら写真を愉しんでいます。
チョウの次はトンボ。今は10ミリほどの小さな虫に夢中です。
虫は種類が多く生活も様々で、歩くたびに新しい発見があります。
ポーズをとってくれる虫たちに感謝しながら、できるだけきれいに
撮ってあげたいと思います。日本列島は秋津洲(トンボの島)とも呼ばれます。
四季がはっきりしていて、春、夏、秋には、それぞれの季節が好きな虫たちが
活動します。冬に虫たちが恋しくなったら、南西諸島へ出かけましょう。
写真には撮る人が写ると言いますので、自分自身も少しでも成長したいと願っています。
虫の説明などには間違いもあると思いますので、ご指摘いただければ幸いです。
今回は株式会社 音美衣杜のおかげで、英文を添えた今までにない写真集を
作ることができました。特に、たくさんの虫の名前が出てくる文章を正確に
訳していただいた山本常芳子さんと、五七五の心を訳していただいた
河内バール八重子さんにこの場を借りて感謝申し上げます。

Japanese Insects and Haiku ***A Photobook by Seisui KIKUKAWA***

Published June 10, 2017

Author
Seisui Kikukawa

Publisher / Editor
Hirotaka Fujita

Design / DTP
Yuko Suzuki

Translated by
Tomoko Yamamoto, Yaeko Barre Kochi

Published by
ONBEAT Corp.
2-2-3 Nakanoshima, Tama-ku, Kawasaki-shi, Kanagawa, 214-0012, Japan
Tel +81(0)44-819-5288

Printed and bound by
SHINANO Co., Ltd.

虫の世界と五七五　**菊川蜻水 写真集**

2017年6月10日 発行

著者
菊川蜻水

発行人兼編集
藤田博孝

デザイン／DTP
鈴木勇考

翻訳
山本常芳子、河内バール八重子

発行
株式会社 音美衣杜
〒214-0012 神奈川県川崎市多摩区中野島2-2-3
Tel 044-819-5288

印刷・製本
シナノ書籍印刷 株式会社

 ISBN 978-4-434-22507-9